Shake Rattle & Roll

Using The
Ordinary
To Make Your
Training

by

Sharon L. Bowman, M.A.

Shake, Rattle And Roll!

Using The Ordinary To Make Your Training Extraordinary

Sharon L. Bowman, M.A.

Copyright ©1999 Bowperson Publishing
P.O. Box 464, Glenbrook, NV 89413

Printed in the United States of America.

Cover design and text layout by Ad Graphics,
Tulsa, Oklahoma.
800-368-6196

ISBN: 0-9656851-3-6

With Gratitude:

• • • • •

The following are friends, colleagues, and training professionals who have inspired me, encouraged me, and modeled for me what training is all about:

Chris Clarke-Epstein CSP, President of Speaking!; **David Meier,** Director of *The Center for Accelerated Learning*; **Tom Meier,** Editor of *The Accelerated Learning News;* **Robert Pike CSP,** President of *Creative Training Techniques, Inc.;* **Sivasailam "Thiagi" Thiagarajan,** President of *Workshops by Thiagi, Inc.;* **Mel Silberman,** President of *Active Training;* **Bernice McCarthy,** CEO of *Excel, Inc.;* **Joyce Duvall,** Administrative Director of *Training Inc.;* **Carolyn Thompson,** President of *Training Systems Inc.;* **Joanna Slan,** Professional Speaker and Trainer; **Elaine Floyd,** Publisher and Owner of *EFG, Inc.;* **Dan Coughlin,** President of *The Coughlin Company;* **Curt Hansen,** Owner of *CURTIS Training Services;* **Karen Hewett,** Director, and **Diane Cheatwood,** Program Specialist, both part of the Faculty, Staff, and Organizational Development Department of the *Community College of Aurora;* **Judy Young,** Director of the *North Carolina Employment and Training Institute;* **Barbara Boyce,** Human Resource Program Director for the *North Carolina Community College System;* and all of the training colleagues and buddies I mention in this book.

Special thanks goes to my mom **Frances Bowman**, for her master editing; my brother **Don Bowman**, for his behind-the-scenes support; my dear friends

Joyce Duvall and **Gene Critchfield** for their thorough editing and thought-provoking comments; another good friend and editing buddy **Cindee "OGMO" Davis**; my best friend and soul-sister **Jan Thurman**, for processing the process with me; and last but definitely not least, my boyfriend **Ross Barnett**, for his insightful feedback and constant encouragement. The title and subtitle of this book would not exist without the wonderful creativity of both **Jan** and **Ross.**

I'm also very grateful to many of **my training participants** who have since become personal friends and who gift me with their "glows and grows," i.e. their compliments and suggestions. And my gratitude to all **my book readers** who email me to let me know how they have put my ideas and activities to use.

*This book is dedicated to
my significant other*

ROSS BARNETT

*who encourages me to
shake, rattle and roll,
and who reminds me
that we are all extraordinary.*

Author's Note:

• • • • •

Most of the specific toys mentioned in this book can be found in the **Kipp Brothers Catalogue** (see resource section for contact information). Other generic toys and learning aids are found in stores such as Wal-Mart, Kmart and Toys-R-Us, as well as stationery, craft, and office supply stores. Please email the author (SBowperson@aol.com) if you have any questions about an item or activity.

Contents

• • • • •

A Parable

• • • • •

When Sally Gluck was very young
she could hardly wait to go to school.
She knew she'd get to learn about
the most exciting things.
She knew she'd have a great time learning,
and she knew she'd be quite good at it.

Poor Sally.
It didn't turn out that way.
She found out that learning
was boring and serious stuff.
Lectures, note-taking, reading, tests.
On and on and on.
She didn't even get to learn about
the things that interested her.
She decided at an early age
that learning was not her bag.

Sally grew up.
She didn't want to have
anything to do with learning.
No more books, classes, teachers.
No more lectures, notes, tests.
Nope, not for her, not ever.

One day her boss told her
that all the employees
had to go back to school
to learn some new skills.
Sally dragged herself to the classroom
feeling very unhappy about the whole thing.

A strange thing happened then.
The instructor told them
they could have a good time
while they learned.
There were fun things to tinker with
and interesting activities to do
all in the name of learning.

Sally felt skeptical.
It was bad enough she had to be there.
Having fun added insult to injury.
After all, Sally knew that learning
was boring and serious stuff.
So, while the other employees
moved about, had a good time, and learned lots,
Sally sat back and refused to participate.

Finally Sally left.
She went to visit her friend, Homer Whettlegg.
Homer listened to her story
and nodded his head. Then he said,
"You learn through pain
and you learn through pleasure.
Period.

If learning is painful,
you'll avoid it, and all reminders of it,
for as long as you can.
If it's full of pleasure and fun,
you'll probably seek it out
and want to learn more.

But if you're used to pain
you'll be suspicious of pleasure.
You won't believe
that learning can be fun,
and you'll be more comfortable
with what you know: the pain.

So make a choice.
You can learn from boring and serious stuff
or you can have fun, play, laugh and learn.
Which will make you happier?"

Sally already knew the answer to that.
She thanked Homer and returned to the class.
She made herself a promise:
she would try new ways of learning
and remind herself
that learning can be fun.

And so it was for Sally.
The more fun she had, the more she learned,
and the more she wanted to learn.
Sally became a life-long learner
and lived happily ever after.
And Sally Gluck and Homer Whettlegg
are best friends to this day.

*With gratitude to David "Homer Whettlegg" Meier
And all the folks at The Center for Accelerated Learning*

Why This Book?

• • • • •

S nap your fingers once. Now snap them on the numbers: *one* and *two* and *three* and *four*. Keep on snapping and say this poem out loud while you snap:

It doesn't take much,
just a signal or a snap,
and my training comes alive
with some rhythm and a rap.

A little rhyme. A toy or two. A blank piece of paper. High fives. Standing up instead of sitting down. Scented markers. A broom. Doodles. Colors. A hammer. Post-its. Pipecleaners. A paper bag. Movement and music.

All ordinary things. Simple stuff. Nothing too complicated or fancy. By themselves, they're no big deal. But figure out a way to include some of them in your training, connect them to the content you teach and the people you're teaching, and suddenly they become much more than ordinary things.

They become the ordinary
that makes your training extraordinary.

I'm not talking about gimmicky learning, or fluff as some folks call it. Or amusing things used solely for the purpose of being funny (although funny is definitely okay). Nor am I talking about trivializing your training.

I'm talking about learning experiences that work for the learners, that are alive with energy and meaning, that make the learning stick long after the actual class or training is over.

Shake, Rattle and Roll helps you create fun and memorable learning experiences. It shows you dozens of easy and effective ways to use ordinary objects and simple training activities so that your trainees learn better and remember more. It gives you lots of practical ideas – some you'll use now, some later. Some may not fit your training style but may fit the training styles of your colleagues and friends. This book enhances what you're already doing well – and lets you know the brain research behind it all.

Even better, this book is also a spark to ignite your own creativity. As ideas pop up, jot them down (that's what the margins and spaces are for in this book – in the middle of a creative brainstorm, hunting around for paper can be a nuisance).

Shake, Rattle and Roll invites you to play. If you're like many trainers, you get your best ideas when you're playing around, "toying" with a project, not taking yourself or your subject matter too seriously. So tinker with the ideas and activities in this book. Mess around. Make it fun for yourself. Then try an idea or two in your next training to see how they work. *And be on the lookout for the ordinary that makes YOUR training extraordinary.*

Play is what I do for a living.
The work comes in evaluating
the results of the play.

Mac MacDougall,
Computer Architect
From: *A Kick in the Seat of the Pants*

Play Break:

On this page, jot down all the reasons why you're reading this book and what you hope to learn from it. When you've finished the book, come back to this page and see if you learned what you wanted to learn. If the book exceeded your expectations (and I certainly hope it did!), add doodles that represent some of the unexpected things you learned.

Chapter One:
Your Secretary Did It

Chapter One:
Your Secretary Did It

• • • • •

L et's start with a simple question: *Do you drive your own car to work everyday?*

And have you ever experienced this? – From the time you leave your driveway to the time you arrive at your work site parking lot, *you haven't a clue as to how you got there!* (If so, keep it under your hat!)

Or how about a time when you've been in a room where you hear a repetitive noise – a clock chiming the quarter hours, a heater clanging away, the traffic on the freeway outside, or the hum of the refrigerator? At first you're acutely aware of the noise, but a few hours later *you would swear that it stopped* because you haven't heard it in a long while.

Ever walk into your living room – you've been there thousands of times and don't even notice the decor anymore – and suddenly you pause to look around, not sure what caught your attention? Then you realize that *something is different.* You look more closely and notice a footstool missing, or a picture moved, or a new chair in the corner.

In all these situations, your secretary is at fault. No, not the secretary who manages your office. It's the one in your brain I'm talking about. It's got some fancy names – "the reticular activating system" or "the reticular formation" – and it's about the size of your little finger. **Basically, it's the part of your**

brain stem that relays sensory information to the conscious mind, and plays a major part in arousal and attention.

How does your secretary work? It only has two jobs (an easy life for a secretary). **The first is to screen out information you already know about** – irrelevant data, stuff you no longer need to pay attention to, routine details you don't need to clutter up your conscious mind with. Your secretary sits back and assures you, *"You've done this a hundred times. No need for you to stick around – I've got it covered."* So your conscious mind is free to take a hike, so to speak.

The other job, and perhaps the more important one, **is to let you know when something is different.** Faced with any change, the secretary jumps out of its seat, bangs on the conscious mind's door, and shouts, *"Come back! You need to be here, now!"*

In effect, it's your secretary who grants you permission to daydream while you're driving. It's your secretary who says you don't need to pay attention anymore to repetitive routines or sights and sounds. **And it's your secretary who puts you on alert whenever anything around you changes.**

Now this is all interesting stuff, especially if you're into brain research, but what's it got to do with training? Let's find out.

Think back to a time when you were a learner sitting in a class listening to a lecture. It may have been an interesting lecture or a boring one. You listened for awhile and then you felt your mind drift a bit. *Suddenly you realized with a start that you*

24

hadn't heard a single word for quite awhile. You couldn't repeat one idea from the lecture if your life depended on it. Where were you? Body was present, conscious mind was a million miles away. The fact was, your secretary let you off the hook with the following advice: *"You've listened to lectures before; you don't need to do it again. I'll hang out and let you know if anything changes."*

So, in spite of yourself, your mind continued to drift. Suddenly you got a mental warning: *"The instructor has something in her hand that she's about to throw at you!"* Instantly you were fully and completely present again. Sure enough, she was holding a nerf ball and announced: *"When the ball is tossed your way, you need to catch it and tell the class one thing you learned from the lecture so far."* Were you paying attention now? Absolutely. With that ball whizzing around the room, you *HAD* to be involved in the learning – no more spacing out. *The ball functioned as a wake-up call to your brain because it was something different from your past experiences with lectures.* The instructor simply used an ordinary throwable object to get your attention and bring your mind back to the learning.

In **How To Give It So They Get It,** I cite a bit of wisdom from a fellow National Speakers Association member and trainer: *When an adult audience sits longer than seven minutes at a time, without doing anything, the minds in that audience begin to drift into sexual fantasy, and no trainer can compete with that!* Now I don't know how true that is – maybe it depends upon the subject matter, or maybe it's a gender thing. But Bob Pike, president of **Creative Training Techniques, Inc.,** makes a similar point in his **Creative Training Techniques Work-**

shop. He reminds his audiences that commercial breaks in television programs occur about every eight minutes. In other words, *as a television culture, we've gotten used to our information being cut up into eight-minute segments.*

That fact alone should warn us as trainers to take a hard honest look at our training delivery. Long lectures, without any brain wake-up calls, are "out." If we truly want the learning to stick long after the actual delivery of information has ended, we need to change our methods of delivery.

> **We need to take our lectures
> and cut them up into bite-sized bits,
> while keeping the flow coherent
> and the connections meaningful.**

Put another way, we need to use a variety of ways to remind the secretary that the conscious mind must be alert and involved the whole time.

What does all this mean when you're actually delivering a lecture to a group of trainees?

> **During your lecture,
> your learners need a wake-up call
> about every ten minutes.**

So you're supposed to toss a ball around every 600 seconds? Nope. **Any ordinary object can be a wake-up call** – and you don't even have to throw it. Household gadgets, toys, props, tools, musical instruments, blank paper, you name it. In fact, **the wake-up call doesn't have to be an object.** Think stories, jokes, skits, cartoons, acronyms, songs, movement, music.

Here's the training buzz word (okay, words) for the wake up calls I'm talking about: **learning aids.**

Simply put, a learning aid
is anything that helps the trainee
learn better and remember more.

Anything that alerts the conscious mind to pay attention is a learning aid. Can learning aids be fun? The more fun the better. Does this mean that your information isn't important? On the contrary, it's crucial. An entertaining training without valuable content is just that – entertainment. Participants may have a great time but not learn much.

The opposite is probably worse. A boring training with valuable content usually makes the participants dislike everything about the training, including the content. To use a familiar metaphor, *they throw the baby out with the bath water.*

What makes trainees dislike a learning experience? My training participants say:

A trainer who ignores our learning needs.

A presenter who's all ego.

An instructor who cares about his subject more than he cares about his students.

A trainer who is boring, sarcastic, or incompetent.

An instructor who teaches in only one way.

A trainer who does all the talking.

Very rarely is something ever said about the content itself.

It makes sense, then, to involve your learners as much as possible in what they're learning. It makes sense to wake up their brains, to add variety to your training delivery, and to use fun objects and activities to keep your trainees energized, motivated, and learning.

Want to know a little secret? *When you do all that, your learners will think YOU are extraordinary!*

Play Break:

Snap your fingers rhythmically and recite the following little ditty aloud:

To make my training extraordinary,
a little off-the-wall,
the learners' secretaries
need a wake-up call.

If you're really in the mood, stand up and move in time to the rhyme!

In the space below, list the brain wake-up calls that you use. Then add to your list any learning aids you've seen other trainers use.

Chapter Two:
Toys-R-Cool

Chapter Two:
Toys-R-Cool

• • • • •

Quickly now, off the top of your head, *say out loud the first five things that come to your mind when you hear the word "toys."*

Were they positive? Negative? A mix? Did they have to do with how you feel about toys? What toys remind you of? Memories related to toys?

At the **Training '99 Conference and Expo** session on learning aids, three-hundred people responded to that question with answers that included: *"Fun, imagination, kids, messy, Christmas, breakable, joy, good times, Toys-R-Us, Toyota (cute!), exciting, cool."* Interestingly enough, almost everyone said positive things about toys. I expected to hear comments like childish, silly, and frivolous. Which maybe proves the point: **Toys are usually connected with good feelings.** And whenever we feel good, we want more of what makes us feel good. I only point that out again because it brings us to the reason why ordinary toys work so well as learning aids. What role do toys play (excuse the pun!) in a training?

- **Toys engage the right side of the learner's brain (the playful, random, spontaneous, metaphorical, holistic side);**

- **Toys help a learner relax and enjoy the learning – like letting the kid inside out to play;**

- *When learners relax, play and have fun while they learn, they learn better and remember more;*

- *Toys act as reminders of information learned, thereby increasing long-term retention;*

- *Toys connect people to people – building a learning community within a training so that trainees can safely share ideas and feelings without risk;*

- *Toys connect people to the training content in humorous yet meaningful ways;*

- *Toys engage more of the sensory modalities – specifically tactile (touch), kinesthetic (movement), and visual (sight) – ways of taking in information other than auditory (listening) alone.*

Sivasailam "Thiagi" Thiagarajan, a corporate trainer who uses games to facilitate learning, said that a few years ago he couldn't mention the word "games" in corporate training circles. Training participants playing games? Ain't gonna fly. Adults participating in review exercises? That's better. Now "game" is a buzzword, and those good at creating and facilitating learning games are nationally recognized for their unique talents. Games are not only accepted but also desired as aids to learning and remembering.

A few years ago this chapter couldn't have been part of this book because the word "toys" was still taboo. Corporate trainees playing with toys? No way! Using learning aids? Well, why didn't you say so in the first place?

By the way, it irritates me when a trainer hands me a gimmicky toy just for the sake of giving out a toy. Actually, my right brain loves it and shouts, "Whoopee!" But my left brain gets upset and protests, *"What's the point?"* So to keep both brains happy, the toy has to serve a purpose.

Toys are simply tools
to make the teaching work better for you
and the learning work better for them.

If your toys do that, great. If they don't, scrap them.

Let's try a little experiment. On the previous pages, I listed seven reasons why toys can be effective learning aids. Without looking back, see how many items from that list you can remember and write them in the margins of this page (no fair peeking).

After you do that, turn back to that list and look it over. How did you do? Did you remember a few?

Next, shorten each sentence in that list into a phrase or one-liner. Write your new list in the margins too.

If you had a bit of trouble thinking up your own phrases, here's a list you can use:

Right brain
Relax and play
Learn more
Remember more
Connect people to people
Connect people to content
Sensory modalities

Keeping your list handy while you read the instructions for the following five activities. Choose one activity to do for two minutes (give yourself more time if you're having fun):

1. Seven Come Eleven: Roll a pair of dice. Now read aloud as many of those phrases on your short- ened list as the combined numbers on the dice (you may have to repeat list items). Roll the dice a few more times and continue saying aloud the items from your list. Do this for 120 seconds. Or you can use a deck of playing cards instead. Choose a card and recite as many items as the card number.

2. Bouncing Around: Bounce a ball in a steady rhythm. With each bounce, read aloud one of the items from your list. Continue bouncing and ver- bally reviewing the list until 120 seconds are up. If you have someone else join you, bounce the ball back and forth between you and have him repeat what he heard you say (remember Robin Williams in **Dead Poet Society** as his students recited lines from poetry while kicking soccer balls?).

3. Animal Toss: Throw a stuffed animal in the air and each time you catch it, say an item from the list. Do this for two minutes.

4. Let 'Er Roll: Write each item from your list on seven scraps of paper and tape them to seven roll- ing toys (if you have kids, matchbox cars will do – otherwise use unopened cans of food). Roll each toy or can across the floor and explain aloud the item written on the scrap as the object rolls. Or use beads: Roll them across a table one-at-a-time while explaining each item.

5. Balloon-Writing: Blow up a balloon and write your listed items all over its surface with felt pen. Now toss the balloon, catch it, and explain out loud one item that your fingers are touching. Continue doing this for two minutes.

6. Build It: With a set of legos, build a simple block house. Name one item from your list as you add a block to your house. Add blocks and repeat items until the two minutes are over.

Time's up. Take a short break. Stand up, walk around, stretch, get a cup of coffee, go outside. When you're done, come back to the book.

You're ready for the last part of the experiment: Without reading your list, see if you can remember the items on it and jot them down in the margins on this page.

Did you do better this time? Did you remember them all?

Right now you may be thinking, *"But I could have just repeated the items over and over again for two minutes without using dice or stuffed animals or bouncing balls."* You're right, you could have done just that. Truthfully, would it have been as much fun? Would it have been as active? Would the kid inside you have enjoyed it as much? Would it have engaged both sides of your brain? Would you re-member the items as well as you do now?

Incidentally, can you think of ways you could modify any of the five activities listed above to fit one of your trainings? Participants could pair up, roll dice, and list a number of just-learned facts. They could bounce balls back and forth while reviewing steps in a program. Working in small table groups, they could roll a toy randomly across the table and whomever the toy comes closest to explains a training concept to the table group. Or they could partner up and build a lego structure with each block representing a piece of information.

You are limited only by your imagination when it comes to using toys as learning aids. Some of the more unusual ones my training participants have thought of are: water guns, fireworks, Halloween costumes, dry ice, picket signs, puzzle pieces, old shoes, funny hats, paper airplanes, play telephones, clown noses, board games, styrofoam filler, toilet paper, indoor basketball hoops, rubber bands, party favors, carnival masks, toothpicks, and paper bags.

Any way you slice it, toys-r-cool. Read on for some more creative ways to use toys to make your training extraordinary.

Play Break:

Create a "Bag-O-Fun" to take to your next training. Take a large paper bag or a pillow case and fill it with toys (deck of cards, slinky, board game, key chain, cowboy hat, baseball mitt, stuffed animal, a set of legos, play dough, golf ball, water pistol, whatever you can find around your house or in your kid's room). As a review activity during the training, have your participants work in smaller table groups. Each group reaches into the bag and draws out one toy. Then each group creates a short presentation covering information they've learned and using the toy as a prop. It makes for an entertaining, energizing, and informative review. (From: *The Accelerated Learning Newsletter*; contributed by Sally Petersen, instructional designer for PNC Mortgage Co., IL)

Draw some doodles here of toys that you've used or that you've seen used in trainings.

Chapter Three:
People Sorters

Chapter Three:
People Sorters

• • • • •

You're a training participant attending a customer service seminar. On top of your handout materials is a miniature deck of playing cards with a small paper scrap that reads: *"Great customer service is like playing with a full deck."*

The trainer explains: *"I come from the gambling Mecca of the West Coast, Lake Tahoe. Unlike the gaming industry, great customer service is not a gamble, but you have to play with a full deck in order to make it work. By the end of this training, you'll have a full deck of customer service skills to use.*

The ace-in-the-hole in customer service is people. You're going to meet the aces in this room by choosing one card from your card deck. Then stand up and find three other people who have chosen the same number or suit that you have. Form a standing group, introduce yourselves, and tell your group what you hope to learn today."

Flash to a safety training for the mechanical division of a large company. The topic is the use of "training tools," i.e. effective information-giving strategies, in safety meetings. On each participant's chair lies a small screwdriver with a colored plastic handle. The sixty participants are directed to sort themselves out into table groups of six to eight, based on the various colored screwdriver handles. They will work in these table groups most of the day.

Skip to a workforce development training. Each participant is given a cardboard shape that, when combined with three other shapes, forms a square. Participants move around the room hunting for the other three shapes. They form groups of four and put their pieces together to make their squares. A question pertaining to the topic is written on each square and each group discusses and answers its respective question.

One more: The topic is leadership. Each trainee holds one of several small animal-shaped erasers. Trainees circulate among the others until they find enough people who are holding the same animal to make a standing triad. Then they introduce themselves and tell how their leadership style is like this animal.

Miniature card decks. Colorful screwdrivers. Puzzle shapes. Animal erasers. All used for the purpose of sorting training participants into random groups. All used to connect people to people at the beginning of a training.

I have a strong bias about opening activities. I passionately believe that the first one or two activities in any training should be about getting connected: *connecting the learners to each other and connecting them to the topic to be covered.* There are sound research-based reasons for doing this.

First, when you connect people to people you create a learning community where trainees feel safe enough to speak out, take risks, make mistakes, and learn from each other.

Second, learners don't enter the room with empty heads. They already know a great deal about the topic you'll be training on. When they get a chance to connect with what they already know about the topic, they'll buy into your information more readily.

> *You show you value your learners*
> *by acknowledging that what THEY know*
> *matters as much as what YOU know.*

People sorters can help trainees begin making these connections. In fact, people sorters don't have to be toys. Counting off by numbers works too. So does grouping by birth seasons, favorite colors or food, years of work experience, distance traveled to get to the training, name initials, number of pets, type of shoes worn, or whatever you can think of that will sort your participants into random groups of the size you desire. The Getting Connected Activities from the books **Presenting with Pizzazz** and **How to Give It So They Get It** are people sorters too. And the simple assignment of learners pairing up with others whom they don't know very well is also quite effective.

But toys add another dimension to people sorting. They can be metaphors that are referred to throughout the training (as in the gambling metaphor at the beginning of this chapter). They can set the stage for "thematic learning," when you choose a certain idea or theme (like baseball, camping, magic, flying, carnival, a murder mystery, travel, a banquet, Starwars, The Wizard of Oz, and so on) to which the people sorters as well as all the activities are tied in some way. And they can represent actual training content (a clacking mouth toy in a communication training, for example).

It's often amazing how quickly training participants connect with each other when toys are present. Smiles, small talk, fiddling with the objects, joking about them. Then, when they discover the toys' usefulness (as people sorters, content representations, metaphors, or elements of thematic instruction), it becomes even more okay to play and have fun while learning.

> *People sorters*
> *connect people to people*
> *and people to content.*

Here are a few more people sorter ideas to spark your own:

1. Porcupine Balls: Participants sort by miniature rubber ball colors into groups of four to six. They introduce themselves in their groups and share three things they already know about the topic.

2. Fruit erasers: Trainees sort by fruit type into standing pairs. They introduce themselves to their partners and explain how learning about this topic is like the fruit they're holding.

3. Plastic tools: Each person chooses one tool from a tool bag and finds two other people in the room who have chosen the same tool. They form a standing triad, introduce themselves, and explain the "tool" or best idea they hope to take from the training that will make their job easier.

4. Colored dots or cartoon stickers: Each trainee chooses a colored dot or cartoon sticker to wear. They form groups of four to six with others who are wearing the same colored dot or sticker. After introductions, they tell why they chose that particular color or sticker and what they hope to learn in the training.

5. Colored 3x5 index cards: Participants find three other people with different colored index cards. They form groups of four. After introductions, they make up four questions they want answered during the training. They write each question on an index card and turn in all cards to the trainer.

Obviously, the people sorter activities don't need to take up much time – a few minutes at the beginning of each training is enough, unless you have some time to spare (ha!) and want to make the activity longer.

Remember to vary your people sorters. If you use a toy at the beginning of your training, use other kinds of objects or activities whenever you want your learners to regroup during the day.

The bottom-line? ***Connecting people to people and people to content is a crucial part of the beginning of any training.*** The people sorter is simply a means to that end.

Play Break:

Flip through some toy catalogues (if you don't have any, check out the resources section at the back of this book and order some free catalogs now). Flag or mark the pages which contain people sorters that you might like to use in your training.

Now skim the catalogue pages again and look for people sorters that directly relate in some way to one of the topics you teach. Mark these pages too. You may not have the revenue to be able to purchase all the items you want, but the catalogue will spark more interesting ideas and you may surprise yourself by creating your own inexpensive people sorters.

Jot down a few people sorters you use or have seen used.

Chapter Four:
Just Toss It Around

Chapter Four:
Just Toss It Around

• • • • •

A koosh throw has been my stock-in-trade processing activity for a long time. Then I had the pleasure of meeting Thiagi, the games expert I mentioned earlier, and I learned the phrase "Random Response Device." Wonderful training jargon! I loved it and have used it ever since. It legitimizes the koosh throw, don't you think?

Not that the koosh throw needs much legitimizing. Most of the trainers I know use a variation of it during some part of their training day.

Basically, the Random Response Device is any soft object randomly tossed around the room for the purpose of generating responses to questions, discussion summaries, idea brainstorming, or information review. Because it's random, and because the participants throw the device *TO* each other (not *AT* each other), the focus is off you and no one feels as if he's going to be singled out by you (by his peers, maybe, but not by you).

As a whole group processing activity, throwing an RRD is one of the easiest ways of showing that you value the ideas your participants discuss in their small groups. You can let the RRD fly for as few or as many responses as you wish (time being the key factor here). You can ask for volunteers who wish to summarize their small group's discussion. Participants will speak up with an RRD in their hands when they never would have spoken otherwise. And all your trainees feel as if what they had to say in their small groups mattered – even if everyone doesn't get a chance to catch the RRD and respond.

The variety of random response devices is limited only by your imagination. Julie Harland, an instructor from MiraCosta College in California, uses four socks (clean, please!) wadded up in a ball. Or how about net bath sponges, stuffed animals, rubber chickens (great around Thanksgiving), Squish Dish (a flexible Frisbee), a piece of fruit or a vegie (not too ripe – and pass it, don't toss it), a funny hat, an inflated balloon (now *THAT* would be interesting), or anything soft and squeezable?

The easiest RRD to throw and catch is a koosh ball – one of those soft rubber-band clusters about the size of your fist that you can find in the toy departments of Walmart or Kmart. Be cautious about using koosh balls with attached hard plastic parts. For that matter, be cautious about using anything with hard or pointed surfaces.

One thing to keep in mind when using an RRD: Many people have never learned to feel competent about catching and throwing. Let them know this isn't a throwing and catching contest. Make it okay for your trainees to miss. ***Let the focus be on the fun of responding this way, not the throwing and catching skill.***

Some activities to do with RRDs are:

1. Pair-Toss: After a pair-share, in which trainees have paired up to share information, use an RRD so that a few of the pairs report out to the whole group.

2. Answer Toss: Ask the whole group a question, give participants a few seconds to tell a neighbor their answer, then use the RRD to elicit a few answers aloud.

3. Group Sentence Toss: Tell your small groups to summarize *in one sentence* the main idea or point from a lecture or small group discussion. Then toss the RRD and have each group state its sentence.

4. Stretch Toss: Have all participants stand and stretch. Then toss the RRD to someone. He shares one thing he's learned so far in the training. He throws the RRD to someone else and sits down. Another person answers, tosses the RRD, and sits. Take as many review statements as you have time for (in a group of thirty people, about eight to ten is probably enough), then thank your trainees and have them all sit once again (a nice way to give them a quick standing stretch while reviewing).

5. Brain Toss: Jessie Tolar, Coordinator for HRD programs at Fayetteville Technical College in North Carolina, uses a rubber brain as an RRD – to "toss a few ideas around." She purchased the brain at Toys-R-Us.

6. Group Mouth: When your trainees are seated in small table groups, each group has its own RRD which is the "mouth" for the group. The mouth is passed around the table to anyone who wants to talk and only the person holding the mouth can speak (the others must listen until it's their turn to hold the mouth). A training buddy of mine made her own group mouth out of a stuffed white sock on which she used felt pen to draw a big red mouth.

7. Prairie Fire: Instructor Jerry Lewis, of Joliet Junior College in Illinois, has his students throw an RRD quickly around the room with each catcher stating a word or phrase related to a topic. The point is to review key topical words and phrases by catching, stating, and throwing as quickly as possible.

8. Celebration Circle: From *Presenting with Pizzazz,* this activity is a great way to end a training. Participants stand or sit in a circle. An RRD is tossed randomly from person to person. Each catcher states something he appreciated about working with the group during the training and one way he plans to use what he's learned. Then trainees give high fives to each other.

Like people sorters, random response devices connect people to people and people to content. Tossing an RRD is another great way to use a toy as a learning aid and to wake up the brain. Remember to vary the RRDs you use, why you use them, and the amount of time they're zooming around.

Finally, keep in mind the old adage (with apologies to apples):

> **A koosh throw a day**
> **keeps the boredom away.**

Play Break:

Look around your house and notice all the soft, throwable things you could use as Random Response Devices. Check your kids' rooms for more. Flip through the toy catalogues too. Write down all the ideas you come up with. Then choose one RRD you've never used and play with it in your next training.

Chapter Five: How Touching

Chapter Five:
How Touching

· · · · ·

*U**sing an assortment of ordinary objects such as toys also delights your tactile learners – those who learn best by touching things.* Gimme a break, you groan. Hang in, I say.

Do you know someone who writes a list of things to buy when he goes to the grocery store, then checks off each item, or runs his fingers down the list as he shops? Or how about a person who encases her daily planner in a pleasingly-textured cover (oh, the magic of leather and suede!) so that it feels good in her hands when she carries it? Or someone else who unconsciously moves his hand or fingers down the page as he reads? How about the person who needs to touch the phone buttons in order to ver-bally repeat a phone number? Or the shopper who first rubs a fabric between her fingers before she considers style and color? These are tactile learn-ers. They need the sense of touch to help them learn and remember.

The fact is, we learn best by using ALL our senses. The more sensory experiences we, as trainers, can include in our trainings, the more chances our train-ees will have of learning and remembering the mate-rial we're presenting. What works for one learner may not work for another. Using a variety of sensory stuff ups the learning ante, so to speak. So the sense of touch isn't as weird as it sounds when it comes to training.

Many of the learning aids you already use engage your tactile learners. Simply by supplying a few "finger-pleasing" objects as part of the training, your "touchy-feely" folks perk up and become more interested. Come on, admit it: Aren't the kids inside us all touchy-feely at heart? And wasn't that our primary way of learning before we were told over and over not to touch?

Here are a few new tactile ideas to try:

1. Note-Taking Tools: Try cloth or paper napkins, small blank paper lunch bags, thick cardboard pieces, slick or shiny paper, ragged torn paper strips, crepe paper, bark pieces, strips of colored and textured cloth, leather pieces, smooth rocks, felt pens of all sizes and colors, crayons, colored pencils and chalk. Link the note-taking tools to a training theme to make them even more meaningful.

2. Touch That Idea: Ask learners to put their finger on the main idea of a handout page, and show their neighbor where they pointed. Or they can touch and read aloud the bulleted items on the page. Or they touch a word and have their neighbor explain the definition of the word.

3. Simon Says: From NLP (Neuro-Linguistic Programming), this is a simple physical "triggering" activity to help people remember information. Trainees touch different parts of their own bodies as they repeat some information out loud. Examples of instructions you can give trainees are:

"Touch your shoulder and repeat the goals of the training."

"Put your hands on your head and tell your neighbor three things you know about the topic."

"Touch your elbow and shout out the most important fact you just learned."

"Pat yourself on the back and tell someone how you plan to use this information."

4. T-Shirt Time: Give learners plain T-shirts and have them decorate the shirts with word and pictures of what they're learning. Then have them wear the new knowledge or skill "to see how it fits." They can explain to each other or to the class what they wrote and drew. They can add to it later or write compliments on each other's T-shirts as part of a closing activity. (From: ***The Accelerated Learning Newsletter***)

5. Frou-Frou Table: The brainchild of ***Excel, Inc.***, a learning technology organization based in Illinois, this is a table in the training room covered with dozens of three-dimensional craft objects, art materials, and household gadgets. Your trainees can use these items in a number of activities or to create representations of things they're learning. The point is to have a wide variety of textures, colors, sizes and types of items you can buy from a craft shop or collect from your garage, kid's room, home or office. The sky's the limit (well, so is training room space, your budget, and the effort you're willing to put into carting the stuff from training to training). Here are some ideas:

Craft Items – *felt shapes, wooden dowels, pipe cleaners, glitter, tongue depressors, sequin, yarn, thread spools, fake flowers, crepe paper, holiday and party items, doilies, beads, feathers, leather strips, balloons.*

Garage Items – *nails, screws, wire, clippers, small plastic or metal containers, paint, carpenter tools, old clothes, string, old magazines, boxes, packing materials, and anything else you can find that's easy to carry and interesting to tinker with.*

Office Items – *paper of various sizes and colors, stapler, tape, glue, paper clips, erasers, 3x5 cards, stickers, file folders, stool, trash basket, coat hanger, coffee mug, scissors.*

And don't forget the play dough, crayons, felt pens, colored chalk, blank paper lunch bags, and anything else that catches your eye and doesn't cost an arm and a leg in money or effort.

If the words "Frou-Frou Table" turn you off, call it the "Spatial Learning Center," the "Training Supply Corner," or "3-D Learning Aids."

What can your trainees do with the frou-frou items? A few ideas:

6. Sculpt It: Small groups use items to create three-dimensional standing or hanging sculptures representing a concept or topic. They explain their sculptures to the whole group.

7. 3-D Metaphors: Small groups, triads or pairs create three-dimensional metaphors for the topic.

8. 3-D Info: Small groups or individuals use the items to add a 3-D touch to chart paper lists of information to be posted on the walls.

9. Who Am I? Each participant chooses an item that represents him in some way, He attaches the item to his name tag. When the training begins –

and as part of the connecting activity – participants explain to each other why the items represent them.

10. 3-D Notes: Trainees enhance their written notes during the lecture by gluing or taping items to their papers.

11. Show Time: Groups use items as props in their skits or role-plays.

12. Souvenir Time: Individuals make simple little appreciation gifts to give each other at the close of the training.

13. Vision Sticks: At the end of a training, each participant writes on a small paper strip her "vision" of how she plans to use the learning, or her dream for herself now that the training is completed. She wraps the paper strip around a short dowel stick. Then she decorates the stick with craft items such as leather, beads, feathers, pipe cleaners, until it's completely covered. Trainees can share their vision sticks with the group in a Celebration Circle if they wish.

Use an idea from this chapter in your next training and watch your tactile learners come alive. I've seen one-hundred trainees cluster around a frou-frou table, drawn there like ants to a picnic. I've received notes from past training participants who said they still had their doodled and scribbled-on paper lunch bags as reminders of what they learned. Others wrote to say they kept their play dough sculptures on their office desks as souvenirs of the learning experience. ***How touching!***

Play Break:

Buy some play dough or Model Magic (available from **Lakeshore Learning Materials** – see resource section) and create your own sculpture representing the essence of a topic or concept you teach. Make this little exercise light-hearted and fun – you're not out to win any art medals. You're just playing with a 3-D medium to see how it feels to do something with art material that is topic-related.

Better yet, have family members or friends join you in creating 3-D meta-phors of themselves. Then have a little sharing session with party stuff to snack on afterwards.

Record any thoughts, feelings, ideas about the experience on this page.

Chapter Six:
Drawing A Blank

Chapter Six:
Drawing A Blank

• • • • •

Know what the most ordinary yet most creative object you can hand your learners is? According to Madeline Hunter, former UCLA professor and international speaker:

> *The most creative thing*
> *you can hand your learners*
> *is a blank piece of paper.*

No way, you say! Here's the skinny:

A blank piece of paper is an unlimited, open-ended, learner-centered information generator. Huh? Let me try again:

A blank piece of paper makes learners work with new information in ways that personally connect them to what they're learning. Better?

Depending upon how it's used, a blank piece of paper can be a left-brain, right-brain, or a whole brain learning aid. With blank paper, you can have your learners analyze and evaluate what they've learned (left brain), synthesize and create new ways of using what they've learned (right brain), or do both (whole brain).

With blank paper, your learners (and you) get to find out what they know, what they learned, what they're still puzzled about, and what they plan to do with what they learned.

With blank paper, you can check for understanding, correct misconceptions, and better modify your training to meet your learner's needs.

Besides all that, activities with blank paper take very little preparation time on your part – no complicated worksheets to make or correct, no running to Kinko's to copy a pile of papers, no fiddling with fonts, spacing, graphics, computer crashes and the like.

Still puzzled about the use and worth of blank paper? Try these activities and you'll be convinced:

1. Blackout Bingo: First, the generic activity. Each trainee gets a blank piece of paper (8 1/2 x 11) and folds it to form eight boxes (sixteen if you count both sides). In each box, trainees write a word or phrase naming something that is part of the content of the training (you have a list of training topics, pieces of information, main ideas, etc. posted on a chart paper or overhead transparency for them to copy from). After filling in their papers (with anywhere from eight to sixteen words or phrases), they stand. While you play upbeat music, they walk around asking other participants to define a word or explain a phrase. The person who defined the word signs the bingo paper of the one who asked him to define it. Participants must go to different people for each signature. When all squares are filled with signatures, the trainee waves his paper, shouts "Blackout Bingo!" and gets a prize.

Variation One: *Do a Pre-Blackout Bingo as a connecting activity. Give them about five minutes. They won't be able to collect enough signatures because they don't know all the information yet. But they do as much as they can. Then, as the closing activity, have them take their old papers and finish getting the signatures to make Blackout Bingo.*

Variation Two: *Use the Pre-Blackout Bingo as a note-taking page during the lecture. Have participants fill in the missing pieces of information. Then, as a closing activity, give them a blank sheet of paper to create a new blackout bingo sheet to repeat the activity.*

Variation Three: *As review, have participants generate the list of words or phrases to be used for the Blackout Bingo activity.*

2. Pass the Paper: Each trainee takes a blank piece of paper and writes her name and one thing she's learned so far. Then she passes the paper to a person sitting next to her. That person writes something he learned, then passes the paper on to someone else. While music plays, participants keep passing papers until they have written on at least five or six papers. When the music stops, participants find their original papers and read the comments written on it. It becomes a review of material.

Variation One: *With each pass of the paper, you can tell them what to write. Examples:*

Write one fact you remember from the lecture.

Write a question about something you learned.

Write the answer to the question that's written on the paper you're holding.

Write one thing you can do with the information you learned.

Write this person a compliment.

Variation Two: *Participants stand and trade papers to write on as they move around the room to upbeat music. When the music stops, or when you give a signal, they find their own papers and sit.*

Variation Three: *Participants stand and form a line. After writing, they pass their papers down the line. The person at one end runs to the other end to pass his paper. They keep writing and passing until they get their own papers back.*

3. Four on the Door: Participants fold their papers to form four squares. They copy the following sentences – one sentence per square – from a chart or overhead transparency that you prepared beforehand:

My feelings about this topic are:

The most important thing I've learned so far is:

One thing I plan to do with the info is:

A question, idea, or comment I still have is:

They write their responses to each sentence, then tape their papers to the doors on the way out to a break. You read the papers and use the information to modify the training and to answer their questions.

4. Ticket Out: Participants write three things they've learned so far on 3x5 index cards and hand the cards to you on the way out the door at break time. You can also have them write questions they still want answered, or what they plan to do with what they've learned (see Chapter Ten for more Ticket Out suggestions).

5. People Hunt: Similar to Blackout Bingo, trainees take papers that they have folded into eight boxes and write something about themselves in each box. Examples: Favorite foods, movies, books, movie stars, vacation places they've gone to, how many kids they have, where they live, when they were born, make of car they drive, etc. Then they stand and move around the room introducing themselves to others and asking if the other persons' favorite things are the same. If there is a match, the other person signs the box. After a time limit, or when someone gets Blackout Bingo, stop the game and find out how many signatures each person collected and what some of the similarities were.

6. Map It: Hand participants blank papers and, as you lecture, have them take notes in a mind-map or clustering form – main idea goes in the middle of the paper, connecting ideas fan out around it with shapes and lines connecting them to the main idea. Doodles or colors can be added to make the mind-map even more memorable.

7. Flip Strips: Cut blank flip chart pages vertically into two pieces. Then cut the pieces into strips about 3 inches wide. Each trainee gets about a half-dozen strips. During the training, the learners write one thought, idea, question, fact, comment, "aha," suggestion, etc. per strip. They can color-code what they write by using colored felt pens. At various times during the day, they tape their strips to the walls (example: questions on one side, comments on another, "ahas" on a third wall) and read all the strips at break time. (From: ***Creative Training Techniques Newsletter.***)

8. Two Part Paper: Cindee Davis, math instructor at Truckee Meadows Community College, uses this type of paper (found in office supply stores) for math quizzes. Students work on their own to solve a problem copied onto the paper from the chalkboard. Then they tear off the top copy, pass it in, and work in groups with the bottom copy to solve the problem again and get immediate feedback as to how they did the first time. Students can also do a Pass the Paper activity with the top copy, then compare it to their own bottom copy when they get it back.

9. Advanced Organizers: Diane Cheatwood, instructor and staff development trainer at Community College of Aurora in Colorado, uses advanced organizers to start her classes and trainings. Participants divide a blank piece of paper into columns or squares and label each division with a heading related to the subject matter. Then they use the paper as a note-taking tool to help organize material as it's being presented or discussed.

10. Musical Questions: Each participant writes a question on a card about the information just covered. While music plays, trainees pass the cards to the right and keep passing until the music stops. Then they answer the questions on the cards they ended up with, using each other and written materials as resources if necessary. They share their questions and answers with the whole group. (From: ***The Accelerated Learning Newsletter***)

11. Overhead Transparencies: Small groups use transparency film instead of chart paper to create pictorial representations of information already learned. They present their transparencies to the whole group.

12. Coin Toss: Each table group takes a large piece of paper (8 1/2 x14, 11x17, or half a chart page) and lays it on the table. With felt pen, the table group members divide the paper into large squares (any shapes will do) and in each square they write a term from the material learned. Then they take turns tossing a coin onto the paper. The tosser has to define/explain verbally the term that the coin landed on or closest to. (From: *Red Hot Handouts* by Dave Arch)

13. Tablecloth Writing: Table groups use colored markers to decorate paper table cloths with words, phrases, doodles, cartoons, etc. all relating to the topic. (From: *The Accelerated Learning Newsletter*)

14. Placemat Writing: During the lecture, participants use paper placemats on which to scribble notes, comments, doodles, and questions related to the topic.

15. Bag Writing: Instead of placemats, trainees take notes on blank white paper lunch bags. They add doodles representing the new information, questions or comments about the information, and examples illustrating what they've learned. They share their bags with a partner, or they can write additional comments on each others bags. The bags can also double as souvenirs of the training.

16. Snowball Fight: This is one of the craziest and most enjoyable activities to do at the end of a training. Each participant writes his action plan – what he's planning to do with what he's learned – on a blank white paper. Then all participants form a standing group in a large space away from the furniture. They crumple up their action plans into "snowballs." When you say "Snowball fight!" they have thirty seconds to throw, catch, and throw again as many snowballs at each other as they can. At the end of thirty seconds, you signal them to stop. Each person picks up a snowball (doesn't have to be his own), opens it, and reads it to the group. If the group is really large, participants can form smaller standing groups of four to six and read the snowballs in small groups instead. (From: ***How To Give It So They Get It***)

Variation One: *If space is a problem, trainees can simply toss their snowballs straight up above their heads, then catch someone else's snowball and read it to the group.*

Variation Two: *Besides a closing activity, the Snowball Fight can be an introductory review activity of material already learned in a previous class or session. Trainees write facts they know or questions about the material. Catchers read the facts or answer the questions aloud as part of the post-activity discussion.*

17. Blizzard Balls: Lynn Jackson, Program Specialist at the Arkansas Career System Partnership of the Employment Security Department in Little Rock, gives the Snowball Fight her own special twist. As a review activity, she directs each small discussion group (or participant triads) to write a question pertaining to the topic on a blank piece of paper. Participants wad up the papers and Lynn collects them. Then she turns her back to the participants and tosses the "blizzard balls" over her shoulder all at once. Small groups or triads catch the balls (one per group or triad) and proceed to discuss and agree on an answer to the question they caught. They present their answer to the whole group after the discussion period has ended. If they get their own question, they exchange it for another blizzard ball.

A blank piece of paper. How ordinary. *And what a simple thing to use to make your training extraordinary.*

Play Break:

In your spare time (!) buy an origami book and experiment with some of the simple folding shapes. Then make up a way you could turn one or two shapes into learning aids. For example, your learners could write on them, exchange them, work with a partner to fold them, or use them as metaphors for the learning.

Note any other far out ideas that pop into your mind.

Chapter Seven:
The Magic Of Metaphor

Chapter Seven:
The Magic Of Metaphor

• • • • •

In **How To Give It So They Get It** I tell the story of my first solo cross-country flight in a Cessna 172. I plotted my course carefully on a sectional, one of those flight maps a pilot uses. When I showed the FAA instructor my flight plan, he was really amused. His comment? *"Sharon, you're in an airplane. Airplanes don't need to follow the roads."* Think about it for a minute – I had planned to zigzag my way across the state in an airplane, following all the major highways, so I wouldn't get lost.

Following the roads is a metaphor for left-brain learning – linear, logical, analytical, moving from point A to B to C, all the way through Y, until you reach your destination, point Z.

Flying an airplane – traveling as the crow flies without the slow step-by-step pace of road travel – is a metaphor for right-brain learning, i.e. learning that is visual, spatial, sometimes instantaneous, ana-logical, *and metaphorical.* This type of learning is like flying an airplane from point A to point Z without having to visit points B through Y along the way.

Left brain training strategies include lecturing, reading, outlining, test-taking. Right brain training strategies include using learning aids, games, storytelling, drawing, **and metaphors.**

The flying story itself is a metaphor, a way of giving you the essence of my idea by representing it with something else. You got the picture inside your head and understood the point of the story quickly, without much explanation from me.

Metaphoric thinking is probably one of the most powerful ways of describing and understanding a concept or idea. The metaphor captures the essence of an idea and forces the learner to "think out of the box," to deepen her understanding of the concept in a right-brain way. And metaphors usually paint mental pictures which stick inside the learner's head long after the classroom learning has ended.

Before you begin to protest that coming up with metaphors is a tough thing to do, let me assure you that we use metaphors every single day. Our daily conversations are peppered with them:

It hit me like a bolt out of the blue.

He's one brick shy of a full load.

She's such a pain in the neck.

It's raining cats and dogs.

He thinks he's the cat's meow.

It's on the tip of my tongue.

She's burning the candle at both ends.

Want to hear a few more? These are from my train-the-trainer participants – some of them even I can't figure out!

That's so Martha!

Through butter like a hot knife.

Sick as a dog.

Blind as a bat.

Skinny as a rail.

Slicker than snail snot (You can thank my friend Joyce Duvall for this one!)

In the hour glass mode.

Dumb as a box of rocks.

A couple fries short of a happy meal.

So bright his mama called him sun.

Are you thinking that all this stuff about metaphors is brain candy? (Hey, that's a metaphor!) After all, you teach technical skills – maybe software programs. Or you train others in accounting basics or systems writing or whatever. So why would you bother your head about metaphors? The envelope please: And the answer is *DON'T.* You don't need to use metaphors at all – *UNLESS* you want to add a right-brain way of thinking about your topic that will help your trainees learn it better.

If you agree that metaphors might have a place in your training, how do you go about creating metaphors that are related to your training topics? Easy:

You let your learners create their own metaphors for the learning.

You set the stage, then let them take over. For example, with your trainees working in small groups (for better creativity), they choose a common machine that represents the topic and elements of what they're learning. They can verbally describe the machine or they can draw it on chart paper and explain it as they hold up the visual metaphor. Let them take it one step further and use their bodies to represent the metaphorical machine (see Chapter Eight for details).

Or ask them a question – "How is _____ (insert your topic here) like a bridge?" – and have them create a variety of answers.

Or tell them to choose something in nature, science fiction, sports, cooking, history, or music and use that item to represent the training topic.

Of course, combining metaphors with learning aids such as toys can be enormously fun and effective at the same time:

1. Finger Trap Metaphor: You pass out finger traps to your training participants. You give them a few minutes to put their fingers in the traps and to figure out how to get their fingers out again without tearing the straw trap apart. They can help each other with this. Then you ask them to name ten ways this experience with the finger trap is like _____ (insert your training topic). If your topic is computer skills, you would say, *"Tell me ten ways this experience is like learning computer skills."* You can get even more specific and ask, *"How is this activity like the computer program you're learning about?"* Their answers may range from the general: *"At first you're frustrated, then it's easy,"* or *"You need your co-workers to help you when you're stuck,"* to the more detailed: *"Putting your fingers in the trap is like inputting the data. Trying to get your fingers out is like getting the data to read the way you need it to read. Tearing the straw trap is like a computer crash when you lose everything."* Get the picture?

2. Balancing Clowns: Each trainee gets a packet of small plastic balancing clowns to put together. The rule is simple: Within ninety seconds (more time if you wish), the clowns must all be connected and free-standing (without human support). After time is called, participants check out the many ways they've connected and stacked their clowns. Ask them to share how this activity is like the training topic. Or they can review pieces of information by stating what each clown represents in relation to its position in the stack and the training content. You can vary the activity by having them work in pairs or triads to create their clown stack.

3. Pipe Dreams: At the beginning of a training, Joanna Slan, author and professional speaker from St. Louis MO, gives each learner a giant fuzzy pipe cleaner (about a foot long). Since her topic is stress management, she asks trainees to scrunch the pipe cleaners into shapes that represent how they feel when they are stressed out. They do a quick pair-share with a neighbor after that.

4. Laser Amazers: At the end of the training, participants wear Laser Amazer glasses while stating at least ten ways the glasses are like what they've just learned.

Variation One: Joanna Slan also uses the glasses as note-taking items. She passes them out at the beginning of the training and has participants write a topic-related word, phrase, or doodle on the glasses at different times during the training.

Variation Two: If Joanna has frou-frou table items available, she asks trainees to choose items that represent information they have just learned. The trainees attach these items to the glasses.

5. Cube Puzzles: When trainees walk in, they receive a cube puzzle with a card that reads, *"Puzzled about _____ (the topic)."* At the closing, they state something they learned from the training which they are no longer puzzled about.

6. Rewards: You can combine toys and metaphors to reward your participants too.

Give 'Em a Hand: Whenever a trainee has contributed a humorous or worthwhile idea, give him a back scratcher and say, "(Name) deserves a hand."

Feather in Your Cap: Jessie Tolar passes out colorful feathers when trainees have participated in activities and group discussions. She tells them to put a feather in their cap.

Tooting Your Own Horn: Jessie also reminds trainees that they can "toot their own horn" when they get a bright idea – and she passes out toy party horns to those who do just that.

Penny for Your Thoughts: Use a bunch of pennies as rewards for contributing ideas. Participants may exchange them for penny prizes at the end of the training.

Worth Your Weight In Gold: Gold foil-wrapped coins (from See's Candy stores) make sweet rewards for active participation.

What if you don't have the resources to buy enough metaphorical toys for your trainees? No problem – try these ideas:

7. Uncommonly Common: Display five common household objects (let's say you choose a funnel, can opener, broom, fly swatter, and hammer). Ask your learners to think of everything they've learned so far about the topic. Then, working in small groups, each group chooses one object as its metaphor. The small groups brainstorm and write down all the ways the learning can be represented by the objects they chose. At the end of the designated time (from two to five minutes), each group shares its object metaphors with the whole class.

Here are some examples of this activity from the ***Training '99 Conference and Expo*** session on using learning aids:

A woman from a software company mentioned that her company's theme is *"Power Tools for a Modern World."* So her group chose the hammer as a metaphor for software applications: *"A software application is like a hammer because you hammer out work with more efficiency, there's no need to beat the computer – you can use it to beat your competition, and it's a new tool to build a solution."*

Another group, with members from a banking company, chose the broom as a metaphor for customer service: *"Customer service is like a broom because you clean up messes that other people make, you sweep money into accounts and sweep problems away, you keep things clean between you and the customer, the bristles work together as a group to get things done, and some of your customers are witches!"*

Variation One: *Put a number of household objects in a paper bag and have each small group reach in the bag to choose a metaphorical object. Or have a trainee choose one object for the whole group to use as a metaphor.*

Variation Two: *Have the participants, as a whole group, brainstorm a list of objects first. Then small groups can each choose one item from the list to use as a metaphor.*

8. Children's Games: Dan Coughlin, President of *The Coughlin Company* and author of *Build World-Class Teamwork,* uses a children's game like Beachball Toss as a metaphor for a topic like effective communication. The beachball represents communication. The ways participants catch, keep, or avoid the beachball represent both positive and negative communication traits. Other children's games can be metaphors for different subjects: London Bridge for steps in a certain process or computer program, Cat and Mouse for problem solving, Tag for internet information.

9. Thorns and Roses: This is a great verbal metaphor to get participants thinking about the topic. At the beginning of your training, direct trainees to form standing pairs. They introduce themselves to their partners, and then share one thorn (the downside or negative aspect of the topic) and one rose (the upside or positive aspect of the topic). If customer service is the topic, the thorn would be the downside of customer service and the rose would be the upside. Use a Random Response Device to debrief the Thorns and Roses.

10. Metaphorical Training Themes: Use an entertaining theme for your training and tie all information and activities to it. Include toys and props (you can make your own) that have to do with the theme. Some of the themes I've seen trainers use are: murder mysteries, baseball, Disney cartoons, ocean voyages, golf, carnivals, safari, sailing, famous people, TV game shows, the Wizard of Oz, surfing (as in "Surfing the Net"), and, of course, gambling.

A few things to keep in mind when using metaphors: **First, everyone must understand the metaphor.** Pretty basic, huh? If you're not sure about it, ask your trainees to explain the metaphor to you.

Second, it should be a metaphor that most people can relate to. Someone may get the context of a computer metaphor but using bits, bytes, serial and parallel ports to represent a customer service program might be a little much.

Third, be somewhat careful of metaphors that are gender-based, culturally-based, or generational. A training buddy of mine recently spoke to a group of high school students on careers. She used the metaphor of LP's versus eight-track tapes. Say what? The puzzled expressions stopped her cold. Right metaphor, wrong generation.

A corporate trainer for the managers of a hotel-casino in my hometown peppered his speech with gridiron metaphors. Football fans loved it. The rest of us sat wondering what some of the points were.

A final reminder: The metaphor is only a part of your information delivery. Even if someone doesn't quite connect the first time, using a variety of ways to explain your information will help all your learners make their own connections to your topic. What works for the goose may not work for the gander. So bite the bullet, leave no stone unturned, and don't put all your eggs in one basket. *Get the point?*

Play Break:

Be a metaphor detective. During the day listen for the metaphors around you: in conversations, on the radio or TV, in magazines, newspapers, movies, your own language. Make a note of any metaphors that you might be able to use in some way in your training.

Think of a concept or topic you teach. If you had to explain it to someone who wasn't even remotely familiar with any of it (it was all Greek to him, metaphorically speaking) what metaphor would you use and how would you use it? Write your thoughts here.

Chapter Eight:
Movin' and Groovin'

Chapter Eight:
Movin' And Groovin'

• • • • •

A nother riddle: *What is the most extraord-inary learning aid ever created?* Let me give you a hint: It's big, it's mobile, it has hundreds of moving parts (got it yet?). It thinks, it speaks, and you can't learn without it. Okay, so the riddle was pretty easy. It's your body. Well, more specifically, your learner's body. And it's the most powerful learning aid around.

I'm not talking about obvious reasons here. Of course you couldn't learn without your body – or at least not without your brain. But what I'm referring to is what most trainers already know: **Engage the learners' physical bodies as well as their minds, and suddenly we have learners who are more successful and who can learn more and remember it longer.** They are, in effect, actively involved in their own learning instead of passive recipients of an information dump. David Meier, director of **The Center for Accelerated Learning,** calls this "somatic" or "whole-body" learning.

Dave goes on to say: *"There has been a serious disconnect between the body and the mind in our culture. We have traditionally associated learning with "mind" alone, apart from the body. But the body and the mind are one. In a very real sense, the mind IS the body and the body IS the mind – one inseparable whole. To deny the full use of the body is to inhibit the full use of the mind. Or to put it in rhyme:"*

If your body don't move,
your brain don't groove.

So movin' and groovin' make for successful learning. Using the body to learn can include activities such as skits, simulations, role-plays, improvisational theatre, and physical games.

In addition to these types of somatic activities, learners' bodies can illustrate a metaphor or can become moving representations of something they've learned.

The best example of this is the computer lesson that Dave Meier demonstrates in his *Accelerated Learning Methods Workshop.* First, he uses participants' bodies to represent the "bits" and "bytes" of computer information. Then he explains the difference between "serial" and "parallel" computer ports by having all participants use their mouths to represent the shapes of the ports (lips pursed for serial, grinning for parallel). After that, certain participants become the bits and bytes: they line up and demonstrate how information goes through the two ports (one-at-a-time "bunny hop" for serial, and all-at-once "can-can dance" for parallel). How about *THAT* for whole-body learning? Dave continues the computer lesson and, by the time it's over, even the folks who have never touched a mouse know more about computers than many of their colleagues who use computers everyday.

Can you think of ways your participants could represent something they're learning about by using their bodies? Try one of these ideas:

1. What's My Line? Each person becomes a certain step in a process related to the topic (examples:

steps in a job interview, a computer program, customer service, a technical procedure). The representations can include movement, sounds, words, action, as well as signs so that the other participants know which step is being represented and by whom.

2. Shake It Up, Baby! Participants work in small groups to create a group sound and motion representing some part of the topic. Small groups present their sounds/motions to the whole group and get wild applause in return.

3. Human Machines: Trainees work in small groups to create a "human machine" to represent something they've learned in the training. The rules for the machines are simple:

Machines can be real or imaginary.

Each person in the small group must be a part of the machine.

Each person represents his part with a movement and sound.

After presenting their machines to the whole group, small groups explain their machines and receive rousing applause.

4. Freeze Sculptures: Participants, either individually or in small groups, create living "statues" with their bodies which represent the topic. Each individual or group presents its sculpture and "freezes" it for a few seconds so that everyone gets a chance to study it. They explain their sculpture to the whole group.

5. Twist and Shout: Trainees work either individually or in small groups to create a song or dance representing information about the topic. Songs can be original or from a familiar tune. Dancing can be done to chosen music or the rest of the participants become the musicians with claps, snaps, etc. (see Chapter Eleven for more ideas).

Ever learn to do something physical, then not do it for a number of years, then come back to it at some point? Notice how, even though you may be rusty, it's as if your muscles remember the sequence of steps while your brain is still trying to put them into words? Put another way – and a good reminder of the power of movement in training – **the muscles remember what the mind may forget.**

Play Break:

Pretend you're in a silent movie where you're giving information to someone but, since there is no sound, you have to do it with gestures and movement. How would you do that using one piece of information from one of your trainings. What gesture or movement would capture the essence of the information?

Ask a family member or friend to pantomime something that happened to him that day. You try to guess what happened before he explains it with words. Then reverse the roles and do it again. Silly? Maybe. But it'll help you find the courage to play more with movement – both yours and your learners' – in your trainings.

Any other movement ideas? Scribble them down.

Chapter Nine:
More Movin' and Groovin'

Chapter Nine:
More Movin' And Groovin'
• • • • •

W*hen you're sitting quietly, listening to a lecture, is some part of your body usually moving?* Like swinging your leg, fiddling with a pencil, twirling your hair, rocking, chewing gum, doodling, folding paper.

Or how about watching TV? Are you usually doing something else with your hands while your eyes are on the screen? Folding clothes, polishing silver, sorting the mail, knitting, sharpening a knife (not too smart there).

If that's the case, you're probably *a "kinesthetic learner," i.e. someone who learns best by doing rather than by watching.* And when the learning situation isn't set up to allow you to learn the way you do best, *your body tries to find a way to move – even when you're not supposed to.*

If you know this about yourself, you can make sure you're prepared the next time you're the learner in a training. Take a small learning aid with you, such as a squeezable toy, a string of beads, a bit of modeling clay, or colored pens to doodle with. If you find your mind wandering, take out the object and play with it (in a manner that won't draw attention to yourself – otherwise all the other kinesthetic learners will want a piece of the action too!) while you sit and listen.

When you hold your next training, conduct a little experiment. Set up the training room so that your learners will be sitting around tables. Then, before the training begins, place a few learning aids in the middle of each table: skinny colored felt pens, a koosh ball, some play dough, colored post-its, a few stickers, animal-shaped erasers, a small basket of legos. Don't say anything about the learning aids for the first hour or two of your training. As you present your agenda in your normal fashion, observe what your trainees do with the learning aids. There will be certain people who can't keep their hands off the objects. Right away, and without a lot of conscious thought, they'll be tinkering with them – maybe making something with the legos or play dough, tossing the koosh from hand to hand, coloring with the felt pens, looking through the stickers. They can't help it – **they're kinesthetic learners and playing with learning aids helps them stay focused and present.** At some point you can tell them about your experiment. And, if you make the learning aids part of your normal training activities, so much the better.

Giving a rather lengthy lecture? (Of course, we hope by now that it won't be longer than ten minutes of straight speaking!) **Engage your kinesthetic learners by sprinkling your lecture with signals** – body movements to show agreement or disagreement, enthusiasm, reactions, opinions, or applause.

First, model the signals and have your learners do them with you. Then ask a few questions about the information you've given them and have them signal their answers. Or direct them to show their approval, applause, and enthusiasm with a certain signal:

☆ ☆ ☆ ☆ ☆

1. Simple Yes or No: Tell your trainees to clap hands once for yes and stomp feet once for no.

2. You Bet: The learner makes a fist, bends arm, and moves it across his chest from one side to the other shouting "You bet." Then he moves arms in an X across chest with hands out (as if to ward off something) and from that position quickly moves them down to his sides, shouting, "No way!"

3. Thumbs Up: Trainees show thumbs up when they agree, thumbs down when they disagree, and they fold their arms when they're not sure or need more time to think about it.

4. Way Cool: Learners raise arms and shake hands above head while shouting, "Way cool."

5. Cool Wave: For enthusiasm or applause, have learners do a "cool wave" across the room, starting at the back or one side and ending at the front or the other side. (If you're not familiar with a cool wave, think about how football fans stand, throw arms in the air and then sit, in a quick succession across the stadium.)

6. Heads Up: To show agreement, learners exaggeratedly nod their heads saying, "Uh-Huh!" on a rising high note. To show disagreement, they exaggeratedly shake their heads moaning, "Uh-Uh!" ending on a very low note.

7. Hip Bumps: Instead of applause, learners stand, raise arms above head, and give hip bumps to people standing near them while they say, "And how!"

8. High Fives: To show enthusiasm or approval, trainees give each other high fives, high tens (with both hands), low fives (hands down instead of up), back fives (pat neighbor on back), knee fives (slap knee and then give neighbor high five).

9. Applause: Magaro Nickson, Sunni White, and the train-the-trainer participants at the Merced County Private Industry Training Department in California, teach their trainees a number of ways of applauding others:

Seal Applause – *Stretch arms out in front of you. Cross wrists, then fold hands so that palms are together. Clap hands like flippers on a seal.*

Adams Family Applause – *Four quick claps and two finger snaps, like the music to the old Adams Family sitcom on TV (or you can do the whole tune with claps and snaps).*

Standing O – *Everyone stands up, forms an "O" around their heads with their arms, and says in unison "OOOOHHHHH."*

Round of Applause – *Clap hands as you circle your arms in front of you, like drawing a big "O" in the air.*

Golfer's Applause – *Stand, swing an imaginary golf club, then shade eyes with hand, look in the distance as if watching the golf ball soar through the air, and say, "AAAAHHHHHH."*

A Big Hand – *Hold up one hand towards the person you're applauding.*

Asking for signals is also a great way to check for understanding after you've given instructions for an activity. You'll be able to see right away how many people understood your instructions and if they're confused about any steps. Simply repeat a few steps, including some false ones, and ask for a yes/no signal for each. Clarify the instructions if necessary.

It doesn't take elaborate planning or complicated activities to keep your kinesthetic learners involved. Ordinary things, like standing up instead of sitting down, can do the trick. Simple things like signals help too. ***And the learning payoff is worth it.***

Play Break:

Think of all the ways you and your friends use gestures to convey messages like: *"that's okay," "not a chance," "huh?" "one more time," "alright," "let's boogie," "not on your life."* Choose one or two of the gestures to use in your next training. Teach your trainees the gestures. Then ask them a question related to the topic and have them answer with the gesture. Keep it light, have fun, and see what happens with the energy level, the mood, and the learning. Record the results below.

Chapter Ten:
I See What You Say

Chapter Ten:
I See What You Say

• • • • •

Think about driving again: *What do you look at when you drive?* The cars in front of you? The lanes to the right or left of you? The sides of the road? All of it? Of course. And even when your eyes are focused strictly on the car directly ahead of you, you're still taking in a lot of information through your peripheral vision.

It works the same way in a classroom or training room. **EVERYTHING becomes part of the learning,** including the posters (or lack of them) on the walls, the colors (what do you think the brain secretary says about hotel beige or institutional brown?), the learning aids hanging from walls, ceilings, or on floors and tables (no learning aids in any of these places? Tsk, tsk!).

Dave Meier calls it "peripheral learning." He says that the brain takes in everything as we learn, everything we see around us, whether we're consciously aware of it or not. So the trick is to put things up on the walls (if you're really brave, hang them from the ceiling) in a training room – things that will wake up the brain secretary and help make the learning stick.

Dave elaborates: *"The mind/body takes in everything in the environment in one gestalt, one sweeping whole, and processes the totality of an experience on many levels simultaneously (both consciously and para-consciously). Therefore, it's very important for the whole learning environment to provide a wealth of multi-leveled stimulation and learning support in the form of aesthetically pleasing wall hangings, mobiles, floor display, and other decorations containing, where possible, reinforcers relative to the learning goals."*

One way to do this is to follow the examples of two corporate trainers, Joyce Duvall of **Training Inc.** and Carolyn Thompson of **Training Systems.** They create or copy one-liners or cartoons relating to the training topic and print them on large, colorful, easy-to-read, laminated (so they can use them again and again) paper or poster board. They hang these puppies at eye level all around the room. I've watched their training participants spend their breaks sauntering around the room, sipping coffee and reading the walls.

Another way to create meaningful peripherals is to print some of the main ideas of the training on large chart papers and hang these up too. The pages are visual reminders of important points and can be used as review later on.

Any visuals your participants create – whether they're lists of important facts or pictures representing the topic – can be taped to the walls too. **In addition, when you display the written work or projects your trainees have completed, the walls become a visual record of the learning journey, sort of a three-dimensional learning journal.**

Here are some of the coolest ways to capture the learning journey on walls – and they make for great peripheral learning at the same time:

1. Gallery Walk: On the walls around the room post chart papers, each labeled with an idea, step in a program, skill, or question about the topic. Play some upbeat "active" music and have participants take felt tip pens and write their own ideas on each chart. Give them about 15 seconds per chart. They can do them randomly or in a particular order. After writing, play quiet "thinking" music and have your participants take a five-minute "Gallery Walk" of the room, writing down ideas on note-taking paper as they read the charts. Then have them discuss what they learned. During the training, they can add comments or ideas to the Gallery Walk charts. (From: *Presenting with Pizzazz*)

2. Graffiti Wall: Hang a really long strip of blank butcher paper across one wall. Label it the "Graffiti Wall." During the training, encourage learners to take felt pens at breaks and lunch times and write their own one-liners and tidbits of information or inspiration. They can also draw their own cartoons related to the topic. At some point towards the end of the training, give the group time to read the Graffiti Wall. If people seem reluctant to write on the paper, make it a "ticket out" where they have to write one comment in order to leave the room during the breaks.

Variation One: Before the training begins, label the Graffiti Wall "What do you know?" and have trainees write one or two things they already know about the topic. A short group discussion can follow.

Variation Two: Cover two walls with butcher paper. Have participants write problems related to the topic on one paper and write their solutions to the problems on the other paper. Follow with a group discussion.

3. The Parking Lot: Label a hanging chart "The Parking Lot" and invite participants to "park" their questions on the chart (either writing on the chart or on post-its which they stick on the chart). Promise them that all questions on the Parking Lot will be brought up for discussion during the training. (From: ***The Creative Training Techniques Workshop***)

4. Wows and How Abouts: Post two charts by the doors. One chart is labeled "Wows!" and the other "How Abouts?" Trainees take two post-its and write a "wow" on one (the most important idea or their "aha" from the training so far) and a "how about" (an idea, question, suggestion, or concern) on the other. They stick their post-its to the charts as they leave the room for a break or lunch. You read over the comments and address some of the "how abouts" in an informal chat session before the training ends.

5. Pluses and Wishes: The same idea as "Wows and How Abouts" with pluses being the positive things trainees have learned so far and wishes being items or questions they want addressed later on.

6. My Turn: Label a chart "My Turn" and invite trainees to post questions, opinions, reactions, ideas – whatever comments they wish – during the training. You can address some of the comments before the training ends.

7. Bulletin Board: For networking purposes, trainees can tape their business cards or 3x5 index card "Want Ad" (example: Wanted – Someone to help me with a customer service project. Contact ...) on the "Bulletin Board" chart. Encourage them to use it to network with each other, to get help or information they need, or to offer help (example: "Great communicator looking to help others solve communication problems at work. Contact ...).

One little perk from using visuals to create peripheral learning: Your visual/spatial learners – those who learn best when they have pictures, diagrams, shapes and colors to look at – will love you for it. So, for that matter, will your kinesthetic learners, because they get to move around as they write and hang things on walls, doors, ceilings and floors. *Happy campers all!*

Play Break:

Just for fun, create a wall space in your office, workroom, or family room where you can write graffiti, doodle, hang inspirational stuff, and play in a visual/spatial way to your heart's content. Remember, this space isn't about "looking good," or "artistic talent." It's about using visuals to play, plan and practice some of the training techniques you'll be using in your next training. So create your own office "Parking Lot" or "Graffiti Wall," "Gallery Walk" or "Your Turn." Invite family members and friends to join in too. Who knows? It could become a really important center of family communication.

Draw a doodle of your Graffiti Wall in the space on this page.

Chapter Eleven:
Twist and Shout

Chapter Eleven:
Twist and Shout

• • • • •

My significant other, Ross Barnett, is a sensory junkie. I call him that because, no matter where he goes, he remembers the smallest details about almost everything – what he sees, what he smells, touches, tastes, and hears. He takes it all in, and can spit it all out when you ask him about it. He's especially attuned to noises – and music catches his attention quicker than anything else. He can be in the middle of a restaurant meal, chatting away with five other people, and can tell you the songs that have played in the background the entire time. Furthermore, he has a great memory for auditory detail – repeating back facts, figures, and data from conversations without having to write any of it down.

Part of why Ross does this so easily is that he's an *"auditory learner" – one of those rare people who easily remember what they hear.* Lecture, for an auditory learner, is like a duck taking to water. For everyone else, though, it's like swimming up-stream without the benefit of webbed feet or fins. Unless, of course, the learner is the one doing the lecture. If that's the case, a quote from **Presenting with Pizzazz** bears repeating here:

The person doing the most talking is doing the most learning.

Lecture is great for the one speaking but not so hot for the ones listening. And if *YOU'RE* doing most of the talking, *YOU'RE* doing most of the learning. That's why it's so important to combine lecture with other ways of learning: visual, somatic, kinesthetic, tactile, **and musical.**

You may already use fast, peppy music during activities and breaks to liven things up. Or you may use soft, slow music during quiet writing or reading times. Maybe you play a song as a one-minute signal to regroup after breaks, lunch, or an activity. These are all great ways to use music to set the mood, energize or calm the group, and do a bit of crowd control.

In addition to that, have you ever used rap or songs to have your trainees memorize some important facts, steps, or details about a topic? If yes, how did it work?

If your answer is "no," here's another of my famous experiments to try.

First, read these sentences aloud and complete them by adding the rest of the jingle:

Winston tastes good _____

Snap, crackle, pop _____

See the USA in your _____

Plop plop fizz fizz, oh _____

Double your pleasure, double your fun with _____

If you were a television watcher way back (ha) in the fifties and early sixties (which, if you're a seventy's baby, leaves you out in the cold), you pretty much knew what came next in the sentences above because they were from the TV commercials of that era. If you aren't sure about the endings, here they are:

Winston tastes good – like a cigarette should.

Snap, crackle, pop – Rice Crispies.

See the USA in your – Chevrolet.

Plop plop fizz fizz, oh – what a relief it is.

Double your pleasure double your fun with – Doublemint, Doublemint, Doublemint gum.

Now think about any jingles you remember from your childhood – poems, Mother Goose rhymes, songs, little sayings that you grew up knowing because they had a rhythm, rhyme, or a catchy melody line. The question is: *Why do you remember them?* Of course you know what the answer is: **Because of the melody, the rhythm and the rhyme.**

Learning through music is probably one of the most powerful and yet largely untapped ways of learning on the planet. Oh yes, much was done in Europe and Canada in the early seventies with the creation of **Suggestology** and its extension, **Superlearning.** A famous Bulgarian psychiatrist, Dr. Georgi Lozanov, experimented with language acquisition while using Baroque music with sixty to eighty beats per minute (roughly matching the human heartbeat at rest). His experiments also included many of the pieces of any successful learning experience: a relaxed state of awareness, a positive attitude, pleasure and play. Unfortunately, not much was done in the United States with Dr. Lozanov's incredibly successful language program. However, out of Dr. Lozanov's research came some of the foundation pieces for **Accelerated Learning** – whole brain, whole body learning – that is currently so effective in corporate training today.

By the way, when I say "as yet untapped," I mean by formal educational and business institutions. Cultures all over the globe have used music to pass down their history and traditions from one generation to the next for as long as humans have existed. *Music still is a universal language that teaches us even if we think it doesn't.* Just think about the stuff teens listen to – and that you listened to when you were a teenager. Or how about your church music and other inspirational songs? Or some of the most famous songs of the American culture? Has any of that music taught you anything about history, tradition, living, loving, values, being human? You bet!

In fact, did you know that singing and speaking come from two different areas of the brain? A famous country western singer, Mel Tillis, stuttered badly when he spoke but could sing words clearly and perfectly. According to Dr. Arthur Winter in *Build Your Brain Power:*

> *Singing is good for your brain.*
> *It makes words easier to remember ...*
> *stimulates a different area of the brain*
> *and provides an emotional release.*

Here's the bottom line: **When you add rhythm and rhyme to your bag of learning aids, you've made a quantum leap in helping your learners remember information far longer than they would have otherwise.**

But you protest that you're not musically inclined. No sweat. Your learners *ARE.* Or at least enough of them are so that *THEY* can create the raps, poems, and songs to make the learning stick. **All you have to do is to give them the information to work**

with, the structure and the time they'll need to do it.

Say you're teaching computer skills and you have a four-step process for them to learn that's part of a particular software program. You first introduce the steps and then have them practice the steps on computers. After that, you challenge them by saying: *"You're going to work in small groups of four or five for about eight minutes. In that time you'll create a little poem, rap, or song that will help you remember these four steps. Be sure to write your creation on a chart paper so we can copy it. After time is called, your group will present your poem, rap or song to the whole class."* After each presentation, have everyone wildly applaud the group. Then, to really ground the learning in long-term memory, have everyone repeat the poems, raps or songs a few times throughout the rest of the training, at breaks, or when walking out the door.

It's that simple.

At the **North Carolina 1999 HRD Training Academy** for the state's community colleges, I facilitated a session on accelerated learning for HRD instructors. I gave them a very left-brain definition of accelerated learning:

**Accelerated learning is
the acquisition of information
in ways that involve
the learner's whole brain and whole body
so that long-term retention is enhanced.**

It's an adequate definition, but not the easiest to remember. So I shortened it, threw in a little rhythm, added three rhyming words, and came up with a right-brain version (you have to snap your fingers in a steady rhythm and say the following phrases out loud in time to the snapping):

> *Accelerated learning means*
> *your body and your brain;*
> *No strain,*
> *memory gain!*

Fifty people rocked around the room snapping and rapping. At the break and the end of the session, instructors snapped and rapped their way out of the room. A great way to use an accelerated learning method to define accelerated learning.

Or how about the definition created by a groovin' group of workshop participants at the **Community College of Aurora's 1999 Annual Teaching for a Change Conference** in Colorado? Led by Canadian professor Kevin Piers from Red Deer College, they snapped and rapped:

> **AcCELerated learning, acCELerated learning,**
> **Uses WHOLE brain, uses WHOLE brain,**
> **ACTtive too, ACTtive too.**

Beth Hendrickson, trainer for American Airlines, changed the lyrics to the Bingo Song (remember? B-I-N-G-O?) to teach transfer policies to AA's new hires. According to Beth, *"This song is used in all the New Hire Training classes throughout AA's reservations system ... the reduced training time is proof that songs can be powerful memory and learning devices."*

A few reminders to get you and your trainees started:

1. Rap is words set to rhythm – the words don't have to rhyme.

2. Poems can be rhyming or free verse too.

3. Songs can be original or set to familiar tunes.

4. The point is to add rhythm, rhyme, or a familiar melody line to important information so that it can be remembered longer – perfection is NOT the goal. Neither is musical talent.

5. Give your trainees permission to play as they create without the threat of criticism or correction.

6. Let everyone exuberantly applaud each other – little prizes to all are fun too.

7. Repeat the musical creations a few times during the training.

8. If possible, have your participants convert their creations to writing and give copies to everyone as a "homeplay" review after the training.

9. The more you experiment with music as a learning aid, the more comfortable you'll be with it – and so will your learners.

I'll say it again: When your learners set what they're learning to music, or make it into a song, rap or rhyme, they'll recall it more easily and remember it longer.

A final note: **Whenever your learners say ANY-THING out loud, even without rhythm or rhyme, their ability to remember it increases.** So have *THEM* do the talking, the whispering, the shouting, the discussing, the singing, the rhyming, the rapping. Have *THEM* turn the ordinary into the extraordinary.

Now snap it out:

> **A little rhythm and a little rhyme**
> **make all the difference**
> **when it's learning time.**

Play Break:

You can practice for yourself (and you'll probably be surprised at how well you do) by taking one main idea from your material, or one small piece of information, and snap your fingers while saying a sentence or two, out loud, rap fashion. Can you shorten the sentences into a couple of phrases? Can you rhyme those phrases in some way? Now get up and move as you rap and snap. If you laugh at yourself, so much the better. If you grab a family member and have him do it with you, you get the prize! Note it here so you won't forget it.

Chapter Twelve:
Making Sense
Of Scents

Chapter Twelve:
Making Sense Of Scents

•••••

Have you ever been someplace, minding your own business, when suddenly a whiff of something assailed your nostrils and *INSTANTLY* you were transported back in time to a memory so clear it might have been yesterday, a memory you had totally forgotten – until the unexpected odor reminded you of it?

Did you know that your olfactory sense is located in the limbic (also called old mammalian or emotional) part of your brain? *Often it's an odor that brings a memory more strongly to your conscious mind than either sight or sound.* The implication of this is fascinating.

I once did a training in an old run-down hotel that reeked of mildew. I don't normally have allergies, but the mildew smell was so strong and I was staying there for a week, so that I ended up feeling pretty sick by the time the training was over. To this day, whenever I smell mildew, I take a quick memory trip back in time to that hotel and training experience. I can remember details of those days (mostly negative, I must admit) because of that odor.

Conversely, whenever I smell chlorine (no kidding), I'm instantly in a mental lap pool swimming happily to and fro, with all the sights, sounds, and smells accessible in my mind. I swim for exercise and feel so good afterwards that every sensory thing involved in that experience (including the chlorine odor) reminds me of the pleasure.

What odors bring back strong memories for you? How about woodsmoke? A certain perfume? Play dough or crayons? Cloves or cinnamon?

A training buddy of mine uses a small electric potpourri pot to simmer a light blend of aromas, usually something natural like vanilla or cloves, during her training. She does this whether she's in a hotel conference room or classroom. She swears it makes everyone feel more relaxed and peaceful as they get to work. She does add a word of warning about flowery scents that may trigger a participant's allergies. She admits she hasn't played with aromatherapy scents yet.

As for me, I haven't actually done my own potpourri field-testing (it didn't occur to me during my mildew debacle) but thought I should mention it here in case you're a brave soul and wish to experiment. Let me know how it goes.

The point is, we DO associate odors with life experiences, and learning IS a life experience.

I'm not suggesting that you get carried away here, worrying yourself into a stew pot about the smells around you. Instead, take a baby step or two towards conscious awareness of odors wherever you are, and try to do something, no matter how small, to make your learning environment more pleasant to the noses that will be hanging out in it.

One way to include the sense of smell in a playful way is to have your trainees write on chart papers with Mr. Sketch "smelly" markers (that's what I call them – "scented felt tip markers" is what they are). Why these particular markers?

1. The smelly markers are a signal that trainees can let the kids inside them out to play while they learn.

2. The olfactory pleasure experienced when using the markers will make the learning more pleasurable – always a plus during any learning experience.

3. The colors are more vibrant than Crayola or other type of markers, and the ends are broad-tipped so that when you write on a chart, the words can easily be seen across a large room.

Dave Meier makes sense of scents by taking it even one step further. To the delight of his trainees, he provides each participant with an individual set of "Fiddlesticks," scented colored thin-point markers to use when they take notes, make "pictograms" (doodles related to the topic), mind-maps, job aids, etc. The Fiddlesticks are also souvenirs of the training and Dave gets calls from many trainees who let him know they're still using their Fiddlesticks back at the workplace (Fiddlesticks are available from *The Center for Accelerated Learning* – see resources section).

Mike Vance, author of **Think Out of the Box,** relates the meeting of his daughter, Vanessa, with Steve Jobs, cofounder of Apple computer. She politely told him that his newly-created Apple computer didn't smell good. When Jobs asked her what she meant, she elaborated: "It smells like burnt plastic. I take scratch 'n' sniff stickers and tape them to the keyboard so it will smell better."

Hmm, scratch 'n' sniff stickers. What if you linked a specific scent to a specific piece of information? Your trainees could inhale peppermint while reciting an important step in customer service. Or sniff chocolate while writing how to close a sale. Or scratch 'n sniff coffee while reading aloud from the company manual (maybe drinking the stuff would be even better). A little weird? Maybe. I'm simply saying: ***Pay attention to the odors in your learning environment.*** Pleasant or unpleasant, they *WILL* affect the learning that goes on there.

In addition to simmering potpourri and smelly markers, here are a few other ordinary things that can go a long way towards making your trainings an olfactory delight:

☆ ☆ ☆ ☆ ☆

1. A Rose is a Rose: Arrange a bouquet of fresh cut perfume-producing flowers like lilac or potted bulbs like hyacinths, or place a small cluster of flowers in an inexpensive holder on each table. You may want to check with your participants about allergies first.

2. Take Me out to the Ballgame: Use a popcorn maker in the training room to make freshly-popped corn as a smell and taste treat.

3. The Percolator Song: Brew fresh coffee in the training room.

4. Odor Eaters: Place small "odor eliminators" that give off light scents around the room.

5. Spray and Pray: Use a light aerosol spray if the room has unwanted odors.

6. Bringing the Outdoors In: Burn light natural-odor incense (vanilla or wood-based) a half-hour before the training (be careful of the scent you choose, and do it well enough in advance so that the smokiness clears and only a light lingering odor remains).

☆ ☆ ☆ ☆ ☆

One final thought to leave you with, from Peter Russell's *The Brain Book:*

The more [sensory] associations
we make when learning new material,
the easier it is to remember that material.

Or to quote an unknown poet: *The nose knows!*

Play Break:

Even if you don't do anything in your training with physical aromas, your trainees can use smells as metaphors for what they're learning. What is the smell of change? Stress? Success? Leadership? Great customer service? Communication that works? Conflict resolution? The technology revolution? What are some topics you teach and the odors that could metaphorically represent them? See what your learners come up with.

The next time you train, be aware of the odors in the room. Do whatever it takes to make the environment an olfactory-pleasing place to be.

More ideas? Record them here.

Chapter Thirteen:
Food For Thought

Chapter Thirteen:
Food For Thought

•••••

Since we're on the subject of smelly stuff, let's take a quick look at the connection between food and learning.

When you're learning on your own, do you find yourself putting things in your mouth? Like sipping coffee, tea, chewing gum, munching snacks, sucking on hard candy, gnawing pencils? Have you noticed that, when you're happily eating or drinking something as you study or work, you take less breaks and seem to be able to concentrate longer? (Then again, maybe the eating and drinking cause you to take *MORE* breaks!)

I'm a learning grazer. When I'm working on a project or undertaking something new, I find myself "grazing" my way through my day. It doesn't help my girlish figure much, but it sure makes the day pass more pleasantly.

For some learners, intake is indeed an important piece of their optimum learning environment. Part of the reason for this is emotional and part is social. Both parts contribute to a learning experience that is more pleasurable and stimulating to the mind as well as the body.

According to Mike Vance,

**"There's nothing like taste
to trigger good feelings."**

He continues: *"Tasting certain foods ... can unleash a wave of thoughts and memories that [affect] current creative activities ... Despite what bean counters and bottom-liners say, celebrating and socializing are important elements in the creative process. Walt Disney and Thomas Edison both made a habit of breaking bread with their teams."*

Good feelings are linked to creative thinking, and creative thinking is part of effective learning.

Ah, but you don't have the budget to go around supplying food at all your trainings. Or, maybe like one organization I know, your company has made it a policy to nix the coffee and doughnuts, not for health reasons, but because it declares that those items are not part of a normal working day so why should they be part of a training you provide?

First of all, you can try convincing the powers-that-be that **providing training refreshments gives training participants the message that they matter and that they are worth the time, effort, and money it takes to provide nourishment.**

Second, you can spend some of your own personal or training dollars to buy inexpensive bags of small snacks such as pretzels, candy, or gum.

Finally, you can have your participants bring in snacks that are directly connected to the topic. Here's what I mean:

☆ ☆ ☆ ☆ ☆

1. What Food Am I? If your training is longer than one day, ask each participant to bring in a small snack to share on the second day. The snack must represent them in some way – it's a metaphor for some aspect of their personality in relation to the topic being studied. For example, in a leadership training, the snacks represent leadership qualities they possess. In a customer service class, the snacks represent the trainees' customer service skills. Before starting the second day, participants quickly tell the group how the snacks represent them. Then all snacks are put on a common table for munching.

2. Tasty Topic: Trainees bring in snacks that represent the topic. Without telling what it is, or showing the snack to the others, each participant describes how his snack is like the topic. The other trainees try to guess what the snack is.

3. Edible Metaphors: Each trainee brings in one piece of food. Small groups combine their foods to create 3-D edible sculptures representing the topic. They explain their sculptures to the whole group. This can be done even with a one-day training – just get the word out beforehand to the participants to bring one food item with them.

4. The Mashed Potato: Bob Pike, in his *Creative Training Techniques Workshop,* uses a potato and straw activity as a metaphor for follow-through. I've used the same activity as a metaphor for any topic I'm teaching. Basically, trainees learn how to put a straw through a potato (yes, it *CAN* be done, but you'll have to call Bob to find out how!) and then generate ways the activity represents the topic being studied.

5. Virtual Food: If it's not possible for participants to bring food, use food as a topic metaphor either verbally ("How is this topic like a hamburger?") or visually (show a chart or overhead picture of a hamburger and have participants generate ten ways it represents the topic).

And a few other ways to use food:

6. Down the Hatch: With participants in table groups, have a small plate of edibles at each table: grapes, strawberries, celery sticks, mini-carrots. Or go for the candy: M 'n' Ms, tiny mints, anything that's small and abundant. Each person at the table takes a few edibles in his hand and then explains a number of facts related to the topic – the number he explains corresponds to the number of food items in his hand and he must explain the facts before eating the food.

7. Rewards: Jessie Tolar has her training participants eating out of her hand. She rewards them with carrots for class participation, great ideas, good scores on tests, you name it. Yes, ordinary carrots. Her learners love it. Working for a carrot becomes the "in" thing to do around her campus. She admits she's also used potatoes and other vegies but says the carrots are the most fun. Maybe it's the color.

8. Gift Certificates: Susan Sobek, Senior Trainer Consultant with the Northern Trust Company, gives out fast food restaurant gift certificates as prizes at the end of the day. Or how about a grocery store gift certificate? They don't have to be worth much – a token amount is still fun to receive.

As I'm finishing up this chapter, I have a hot cup of tea steaming by one side of my computer, a small bowl of chips near the other, and the dinner casse-role aroma wafting my way from the kitchen close by. "A loaf of bread, a jug of wine ..." Ah, a learning paradise from ordinary edible things!

Play Break:

Take a poll. Find out how many of your training friends like to have food around while they learn, teach, or train. Ask them what they do about providing snacks and the like for their trainees. Do they use food as a learning aid and, if so, how? Doodle some food ideas below.

Chapter Fourteen:
Crowd Control

Chapter Fourteen: Crowd Control

• • • • •

You've got your trainees rappin' and rhymin' their way through your training. You've held snowball fights, ball toss games, and blackout bingos. You've used toys as metaphors and your learners' bodies to demonstrate important points. And through it all you've been faced with the same problem: ***How in the world do you get their attention again (and in a timely fashion) once you've turned them loose to shake, rattle and roll?***

Ah, the trainer's worst nightmare – a room full of adults totally out of control! No wonder so many of us opt for the safer shallows when treading the training waters of learner-centered instruction. Keep 'em seated, keep 'em relatively quiet, keep 'em focused on us and not on each other. All effective ways of crowd control. And all pretty ineffective ways of learning if we truly want our training participants to leave with information and skills *they can use.*

What to do?

• ***Teach a group management technique before you begin the training;***

• ***Have a group management tool ready to use that is a strong enough wake-up call to which every trainee will pay immediate attention.***

Let's take a look at group management tools that fit these two suggestions.

1. Noisemakers: Explain to your participants before an activity that, when they hear a certain noise, they need to stop what they're doing and turn their attention back to you for the next activity. Noisemakers can be simple toys like whistles, horns, slide flutes, kazoos. They can be household objects like a wind chime, a spoon and water glass, or a bunch of jingling keys. Or they can be training tool noises like tapping the microphone. Be sure to practice using your noisemaker before a training to make sure the sound is loud enough without being annoying.

2. Music: Have a "signature" piece of music that always represents: "Stop what you're doing and turn your attention this way." Explain the music signal before the first activity. You can also use percussion instruments like a tambourine, a set of bongos, or a bell. Or play an easily portable musical instrument such as a recorder or flute.

3. Visual Signals: Explain to your trainees that, when you raise your hand, they need to stop talking and raise their own hand also. Or hold up a brightly- colored large paper with the following sentence printed big and bold: "If you can see this, stop and turn this way." Or walk around with a pre-made sign in your hand. The sign says: "One minute to finish," or "When you're finished, sit down," or "If you can read this, stop and look at me," or "Times up – have a seat."

4. Clap or Snap: When an activity is over, Bob Pike says quietly to the group, "If you can hear my voice, clap once. If you can hear my voice, clap twice. If you can hear my voice, clap three times." By that time, the whole group is clapping and he has the attention of all.

Variation One: Instead of clapping, say, "If you can hear my voice, snap once, snap twice, snap three times." Or, "If you can hear my voice, raise one hand, raise another, nudge your neighbors if their hands aren't up, wiggle your fingers." Or "If you can hear my voice, stomp once, twice, three times." The variations are endless.

Variation Two: Teach your training participants to clap "Shave and a Hair Cut – Two Bits" (five claps, pause, then two more). Let them know that, whenever you do the first five claps, they need to stop what they're doing and do the last two claps. Practice it a couple of times to make sure they understand. Then use the five claps as your signal to pay attention, and they'll respond with the two claps to show you they're ready.

5. Lights Out: If you have easy access to a light switch, flick them off to get the attention of the group.

6. Secret Word: Let the group choose a secret word for the day. The word needs to be one that wouldn't normally come up in conversation (nonsense words or unusual words work well; so does a word that is topic related). Whenever they hear or see this word, they whisper it to their neighbors, then stop and listen.

Remember the brain secretary? Sometimes too much of one group management signal and you'll find that your learners cease to pay attention (it's "the same-old thing" syndrome). So you may want to vary the group management tools you use (let's hear it for brain wake-up calls!). Or put your learners in charge of creating methods to get the group's total attention.

Whatever you do, the cardinal rule is *NOT* to shout above your trainees voices (and believe me, I've done that so many times I could get an award). Ultimately it just escalates the noise.

One other no-no: **Don't ignore your own attention-getting signal.** I can't tell you how many times I've raised my hand or sounded a noisemaker and then continued talking to a trainee while waiting for everyone else to quiet down. Not exactly the best modeling of the behavior I want from my trainees.

Remember to be a little flexible with the time it takes to settle down. **Anytime you engage learners in activities, they will need some start up and wind down time.** It's all part and parcel of interactive learning.

The more comfortable you are with a variety of creative ways to regain the focus of the group, the more your trainees will pay attention to your group management tools. Their brain secretaries will want to know, *"Well what is she going to do next to get our attention?"* At that point, crowd control will no longer be an issue for you. You'll have them eating out of your hand – oops! Wrong metaphor for this chapter! Let's see: They'll be all ears – and eyes too!

Play Break:

I know you've seen many crowd control techniques – and you've used quite a few yourself. Jot them down and add any new ones to the list. Then try out something you've never done before and write down the results.

Chapter Fifteen:
The Power Of
The Ordinary

Chapter Fifteen:
The Power Of The
Ordinary

• • • • •

Up until this point, you've been reading about ordinary things that make learning experiences more successful for your training participants. Now let's switch gears for a chapter and take a look at real things that create a feeling of emotional well-being for YOU – **ordinary things that help you refocus, re-energize, and feel good about yourself and your work.**

But first, a story (a Bowmanized version of an old tale): *It was a hot day, the training had been a long one, and trainees were tired and thirsty. The trainer took a pitcher of water and began filling the participants' water glasses. Soon the pitcher was empty but the trainer continued to pour nothing into empty glasses. Finally, a trainee spoke up: "Excuse me, but your pitcher is empty. You need to refill it first before you fill our glasses." The trainer looked at him and smiled. "You're absolutely right." She then left to refill her pitcher.*

So what refills your pitcher? What little ordinary things support you as you train? What keeps your energy moving and flowing so that you can fill the water glasses of your learners without depleting your own? **What is the ordinary stuff that renews and re-energizes YOU?**

During the training itself, the things that refill your pitcher could simply be the excitement and success of your learners, their enthusiasm and positive comments both verbally and on evaluation forms, your client's satisfaction, and a job well done.

You could also include little things that make you feel comfortable: a glass of water, colorful peripherals, materials organized and ready to go, a little extra time before everyone arrives so that you can relax, stretch breaks (literally), your favorite Random Response Device, snack food, mood music, a new set of colored felt pens, a fun opening activity that gets you connected to your trainees, a story you enjoy sharing (that's related to the training topic, of course).

How about before the training? A good night's sleep (sometimes impossible but a great goal anyway). And probably the most important stuff is that which you ingest – healthy food which will keep you alert the longest (nix the caffeine and sugar if you can). Of course, allowing for extra prep time to take care of last minute details and problems that often arise is a great gift to give yourself. Even better is a training schedule that allows for a little down time the morning of or evening before the training begins. For many of my colleagues, that in itself is a major luxury.

After the training, pay attention to what your body needs as well as your mind. Maybe a walk, a nap, or some hot tub time is in order. A change of pace or escape into a novel or a movie. Maybe something as simple as listening to your favorite music, a glass of fine wine, dinner with friends or family, playing with kids (yours or the neighbors), dancing, or reading the newspaper.

While you're figuring out what re-energizes you after a training, don't forget the small things that make a hotel room a home (if you're an on-the-road trainer). Or if you don't travel to train, do you have a small space in your office or home that you use to help you refocus and relax? Don't underestimate the power of a green plant in a pretty basket, a vase of colorful flowers, a perfume, cologne, or scented candle you enjoy, a special photo, a momento that means a lot to you, an inspirational quote, a cozy quilt, a soft pillow, a personalized notebook, a stuffed animal (don't laugh – the kid in you once got a lot of comfort from them), a spiritual icon, a room with a view, a quiet place.

Let's face it – it's easier to think about what will work for our trainees than to take the time to figure out what works best for us. And in all the hustle and bustle of training, it's often the norm to forget to nurture our own bodies and minds. We convince ourselves that the crazy schedules are okay, that we'll bop until we drop, that we'll take a vacation after all the work gets done, and that we'll take care of ourselves *when we have the spare time to do so.*

What I'm suggesting here is that we begin with the little things – baby steps in the direction of a healthier way of being while we're helping others learn. When we focus on the pleasure something small can give us, we allow ourselves – however briefly – to relax and reclaim some of the energy we've lost in the work.

I can lecture to myself forever about the radical changes I need to make in my life: daily exercise, a healthy diet, maintaining a close support system, organizing my time and work space, growing my business, managing my stress. Nothing changes.

Or if it does, the changes are short-lived. Taken together, the tasks are too big, the changes too monumental, the effort demanded of me too great. For me, when I see the big picture, I panic.

But focusing on something small and ordinary, right in front of my eyes, helps me regain my balance. For example, right now, at this very moment, while I'm sitting at the computer typing this very sentence, I can ask myself: *"What little thing can I do that will nurture myself?"* And the answer comes easily: I can stretch my back and drink a glass of water. And then I can take a very short break, step outside, and breathe in the fresh morning smells of woods, moist earth, and sunshine. *I'll be right back ...*

Play Break:

It's your turn now. Ask yourself, *"At this very moment, what little thing can I do that will nurture myself and make me feel good?"* Then get up and do it.

As you go through your day, become aware of the little things that give you pleasure. Stop to notice them. Give thanks for them. Consciously begin to include more of them with each day.

Draw some doodles on this page that represent the ordinary things that nurture you.

Chapter Sixteen:
YOU Are Extraordinary

Chapter Sixteen:
YOU Are Extraordinary

• • • • •

Picture yourself as a training participant. You just finished taking part in a day-long workshop on using the ordinary to make your training extraordinary. The trainer has directed you and the other twenty trainees to form a standing circle in the back of the room. Holding a Random Response Device in her hand, she asks, *"What do you think you've been learning about all day?"* You and the other participants toss the RRD around as you answer:

- *Using ordinary objects as learning aids.*

- *Using people sorters to connect people to people and people to content.*

- *Reviewing with Random Response Devices.*

- *Ways to include tactile learning.*

- *Creating metaphors that help make the learning stick.*

- *How to do more kinesthetic learning.*

- *The power of a blank piece of paper.*

- *What peripheral learning is all about.*

- *Using rhythm and rhyme to help learners remember longer.*

- *Sensory learning such as smell and taste.*

- **Methods of crowd control.**

- **Using objects, ideas and activities to help trainees learn better and remember more.**

"You're absolutely right," the trainer agrees. Then she glances over her shoulder and around the room as if to check for any eavesdroppers about. She lowers her voice, leans into the circle, and whispers, *"Do you want to know a very special secret?"* You nod your head and lean in so you can hear her words. She continues:

Here is the special secret:
This learning experience has been about YOU.
YOU are what makes your training
extraordinary.

I don't mean YOU as a skilled trainer,
or a giver of important information.
I mean YOU as a sharer of energy,
of spirit, of being.

WHO YOU ARE
teaches your learners far more
than what you say.
WHO YOU ARE
stays with your trainees far longer
than the words you speak.

For better or worse,
they will become more
Of who THEY are
because of who YOU are.

Well, after that you feel pretty darn good – so you give some high fives (and maybe a hip bump or two) to the other training participants. Because the fact of the matter is – it's true! **During a training, you share your time, talent, energy and SPIRIT with your trainees.** They soak *YOU* up, so to speak, and carry a bit of you with them when they leave. And if you're really good, they not only want more of your message but more of your energy too.

A famous trainer (who shall remain nameless) once told me that a trainer's information should stand independently from the person delivering the information. The concepts and ideas are what should be remembered, not the trainer. My thought on that? A lot of baloney! This particular trainer is famous first because of *WHO SHE IS*, and second because of *WHAT HER MESSAGE IS*. **Her authenticity as a human being, and passion for what she believes in, makes her message credible.** It doesn't happen the other way around.

The point I'm making? **You don't have to be anyone else. You only have to be YOU.** You with your ego set aside for awhile, you with your most authentic self, your highest truth, your spirit and passion and energy shining forth. That's first.

You don't have to be perfect. You don't have to have all the answers. You don't have to make sure that everyone likes you. You don't have to have all sorts of credentials. You don't have to stand on a pedestal.

**Your trainees come to you hungry –
physically, mentally, emotionally, spiritually.
Give them a little food
to feed them on all levels.**

Give them a training that connects them to one another and makes them feel good about themselves as learners – that's emotional food. Give them ideas that challenge their minds and some practice time with skills they can use. That's mental and physical food. *And give them your passion and your vision for what they can become because of the time they spent learning with you and each other.* That's spiritual food.

And while you're feeding them on all those levels, **LET THEM PLAY!** Keep them motivated and alert with brain wake-up calls. Include learning aids to help them learn better and remember more. Use all sorts of ordinary things to make your training extraordinary. And most importantly:

Give them yourself,
extraordinary you,
to learn from
and grow with,
so that they, too,
can become extraordinary.
Then go out and
shake, rattle and roll!

About The Author

•••••

Sharon Bowman, M.A., wears a lot of hats (notice the metaphor?). Among other things, she is:

- a Fortune 500 and workforce development **trainer**
- a part-time community college **instructor**
- the **owner** of Bowperson Publishing Company
- a **member** of the National Speakers Association
- the **director** of The Tahoe Training Design Experience

She is passionate about interactive, learner-centered training design and delivery. She helps organizations fine-tune their staff development programs and create new ways of learning for maximum training transfer. She is the author of two successful training books, *Presenting With Pizzazz,* and *How To Give It So They Get It,* as well as numerous magazine and newsletter articles on teaching and learning. You can contact her for a complete description of seminars and workshops as well as information about her newest project, *The Tahoe Training Design Experience.* She also welcomes your training ideas and stories for possible inclusion in her next book, *From Sage-on-the-Stage to Guide-on-the-Side: Changing the Training Paradigm.*

Sharon L. Bowman, M.A.
Author and Trainer
P.O. Box 464, Glenbrook, NV 89413
Phone and Fax: 775-749-5247
Email: SBowperson@aol.com
Website: Bowperson.com

About The Author's Books

•••••

Presenting with Pizzazz

*"This perky little paperback by an **Accelerated Learning Workshop** graduate contains a host of easy-to-apply ideas for getting learners more actively involved in their own classroom-based learning ... in style and content, a gem of a book."*

Tom Meier, Editor
The Accelerated Learning Newsletter

*"**Presenting with Pizzazz** is full of high energy activities designed to get participants on their feet while they learn. The author's experience, energy, and sense of humor are clearly revealed on every page of the book."*

Sivasailam "Thiagi" Thiagarajan, Editor
Thiagi Game Letter

How To Give It So They Get It

*"Using the metaphor of flying and based solidly in learning styles research, **How To Give It So They Get It** shows you in vivid language how to design training in a way that consistently reaches all learning styles...a superb book and a must for any trainer."*

Tom Meier, Editor
The Accelerated Learning Newsletter

You can order Sharon Bowman's books at your local bookstore, through the training company and catalogue websites listed in the resource section of this book, from amazon.com, or by contacting *Bowperson Publishing* directly at **775-749-5247.**

Resources

Just The FAQs

· · · · ·

The following are some of the frequently-asked-questions from my train-the-trainer workshops. **There are no "right" answers.** There are only yours, mine, or other trainers' answers. Because I'm the designated author here, I get to give you *MY* answers (lucky me). If they feel good to you, fine. If they don't make any sense to you, skip them and come up with your own. Better yet, send me *YOUR* answers so that, the next time around, I can include them in a chapter like this. Even better than that, *write your OWN training book!*

Q: What if a trainee thinks that the learning aids or activities are silly and refuses to do them?

A: To prepare my training participants for hands-on learning, I introduce them to four basic ideas before the training begins:

1. They will be learning some great information in some fun new ways and I invite them to "stretch" a little out of their "comfortable places," i.e. the ways they've been used to learning.

*2. I show them the following quote (from **Presenting with Pizzazz**): "The person doing the most talking – or moving or writing – is doing the most learning." I tell them THEY will be doing the most talking, moving and writing, not me.*

3. If someone feels she has "stretched" enough, she can choose to be an observer for awhile. That way, the power is given back to the learner to take care of her own learning needs.

4. There IS method to the madness. There IS a brain-based reason for doing each activity or using each learning aid. I will let them know the learning objective so that they understand the purpose behind the method.

Most of my trainees are usually willing to learn in new ways then. Some people just need your permission to let their hair down and play. Others will need some time to ease into having fun while learning. And some may opt just to watch – and that's okay too.

When all is said and done, you need to be okay with the fact that you're *NOT* going to please everyone all the time. There *WILL* be some people who won't like *ANYTHING* you do. Others may feel a little threatened by new ways of learning – after all, it's been done lecture-style for so long. That's what they're comfortable with even if it does bore them. And some people truly learn better by themselves, at least for awhile. **Let people do what they need to do as long as they don't dampen the learning experience for the others.**

Q: What if they do just that? What if there is someone who is very vocal about his dissatisfaction?

A: Here's my mantra: **NEVER sacrifice the group for the individual.** I say that only because I've done it dozens of times and have always regretted it.

Now I try to do it differently. I call for a break and talk privately with the person to find out what's going on. I do a little "active listening," repeating back what he's said and asking some clarifying questions. Then I state what I see happening in the training and how it's affecting the learning of the others. I try to find options that will work for both the dissatisfied person and the group. Sometimes just this private chat does the trick (for more information on dealing with difficult participants, see Bob Pike's book in the resource section).

The hardest part for me is this: I've got to give myself permission to say to a negative trainee, *"Maybe this isn't the best place for you to be right now. Maybe this isn't the right time for you to be attending this training."* I've got to give myself permission to ask a trainee to leave, if it comes to that. I'm not there yet, but that's what I'm aiming for, so that the group isn't sacrificed for the one.

Q: Can you overdo it with learning aids?

A: Absolutely! Remember the brain secretary? Use the same learning aids over and over and your participants will stop paying attention. Conversely, use too many learning aids in too short a time, and the brain secretary goes on overload. It tells the conscious mind to shut down because there's just too much to deal with. Sort of a stress-reaction to over-stimulation.

The solution? There's no hard and fast rule of thumb, and a lot of it has to do with your own comfort in using learning aids. When I first started training, I used one or two learning aids an hour (maybe a people sorter and a random response device). Now I use one about every ten minutes but for different purposes (a blank paper for note-taking, a metaphor to represent the main idea, doodle drawings in addition to writing, a story to illustrate a point, a short game and a gallery walk to review material). *Remember that learning aids aren't just toys and other objects – they can be activities, pictures, stories, songs, doodles, jokes, etc. So vary your learning aids in ways that won't freak out the ever-vigilant brain secretary.*

Q: Where can I get more ideas for learning aids and leaner-centered activities?

A: The companies I've listed in the resource section offer a variety of training products and services based on interactive training design and delivery. Of course you can always buy *Presenting with Pizzazz* and *How To Give It So They Get It* (not just because the author is a very close friend of mine, but because the books are learner-centered with dozens of useful ideas and activities). Finally, your own training buddies are wonderful resources – stay in touch and trade ideas back and forth.

If you have a question you want my thoughts about, or a training story you would like to share, please email it to me – SBowperson@aol.com – and I'll reply ASAP. Good luck and happy training!

Sharon L. Bowman, M.A.
Author and Trainer
P.O. Box 464
Glenbrook, NV 89413
Phone and Fax: 775-749-5247
Email: SBowperson@aol.com
Website: Bowperson.com

Trainers and Training Companies

•••••

Suppliers of excellent training products and services, including in-house training programs and public seminars. Call for more information.

Active Training, Inc.
Mel Silberman, President
26 Linden Lane, Princeton, NJ 08540
Phone: 609-924-8157   Fax: 609-924-4250
Website: activetraining.com

Career Point, Inc.
Ralph Kraus, Training Director
4150 Belden Village St. NW, Canton, OH
Phone: 877-212-1689   Fax: 330-492-9012

The Center for Accelerated Learning
David Meier, Director
1103 Wisconsin St., Lake Geneva, WI 53147
Phone: 414-248-7070   Fax: 414-248-1912
Website: www.execp.com/~alcenter

The Coughlin Company
Dan Coughlin, President
P.O. Box 21814, St. Louis, MO 63109
Phone: 314-453-8453   Fax: 314-638-3485

CURTIS Services
Curt Hansen, Owner
5160 West Jackson Road, Elwell, MI 48832
Phone: 517-887-8410

Creative Training Techniques International, Inc.
Robert Pike, CSP, President
7620 West 78th St., Minneapolis, MN 55349
Phone: 800-383-9210   Fax: 612-829-0260
Website: www.cttbobpike.com

Excel, Inc.
Bernice McCarthy, CEO
23385 Old Barrington Road, Barrington, IL 60010
Phone: 800-822-4628   Fax: 847-382-4510
Website: www.excelcorp.com

EFG Inc. (formerly **Newsletter Resources**)
Elaine Floyd, Publisher and Owner
6614 Pernod Ave., St. Louis, MO 63139
Phone: 800-264-6305   Fax: 314-647-1609
Website: www.newsletterinfo.com

Speaking!
Chris Clarke-Epstein, CSP, President
P.O. Box 37, Wausau, WI 54945
Phone: 715-842-2467   Fax: 715-848-9463

Training, Inc.
Joyce Duvall, Administrative Director
47 South Pennsylvania, Suite 801,
Indianapolis, IN 46204
Phone: 317-264-6740   Fax: 317-264-6738

Training Systems, Inc.
Carolyn Thompson, President
221 Vermont Road, Frankfort, IL 60423
Phone: 815-469-1162   Fax: 815-469-0886

Workshops by Thiagi
Sivasailam "Thiagi" Thiagarajan, President
4423 E. Trailridge Rd., Bloomington, IN 47408
Phone: 800-996-7725   Fax: 812-332-5701
Website: thiagi.com

Joanna Slan, Professional Speaker
7 Ailanthus Court, Chesterfield, MO 63005
Phone: 800-356-2220   Fax: 314-530-7970

Newsletters

• • • • •

Accelerated Learning Application News (414-248-7070). Editor: Tom Meier. Publisher: The Center for Accelerated Learning. The most practical and usable newsletter for trainers and teachers of any content area – packed with how–to ideas, tips, and techniques as well as excellent updates on accelerated learning. A must for any trainer.

Creative Training Techniques Newsletter (800-707-7749). Editor: Bob Pike. Publisher: Lakewood Publications. Another great newsletter for trainers who want practical ideas that can be used immediately with little preparation time.

Thiagi Game Letter (888-378-2537). Editor: Sivasailam "Thiagi" Thiagarajan. Publisher: Jossey-Bass/Pfeiffer. An excellent resource for a variety of "game" ideas and activities, including a "framegame" with each issue.

Catalogues

• • • • •

The Brain Store Catalogue (619-546-7555). A collection of the best books around on teaching, learning, and brain research; also includes some unusual brain-related items.

Creative Training Techniques Catalogue (800-383-9210). A great assortment of training books and learning aids; especially for the busy trainer who wants some shortcuts in preparation time.

Jossey-Bass/Pfeiffer Catalogue (800-274-4434). A large variety of books, VHS tapes, and other training resources.

Kipp Brothers Catalogue (800-426-1153). The best assortment of wholesale toys I have found anywhere – with the best quantity pricing. Most of the specific toys and metaphoric learning aids in this book are from *Kipp Brothers.*

Lakeshore Learning Materials (800-421-5354). Supplier of children's educational toys including "Model Magic," a unique white sculpting material participants can write on.

Oriental Trading Company (800-228-2269). Unusual toy and craft items that can be bought in bulk. Prices are higher than *Kipp Brothers.*

Spilsbury Puzzle Company (800-772-1760). Unique but pricey puzzles, games, and gifts – their pocket-size portable "dexterity" puzzles make for nice metaphoric gifts, as do their metal brain twisters.

The Trainer's Warehouse Catalogue (800-299-3770). A fun and eclectic collection of products especially selected and developed to make training more hands-on and learner-centered.

Brain Research Books:

• • • • •

Armstrong, Thomas. **Seven Kinds of Smart: Identifying and Developing Your Many Intelligences.** Plume, NY 1993

Gardner, Howard. **Multiple Intelligences: The Theory in Practice.** Basic Books, NY. 1993

Hannaford, Carla. **Smart Moves: Why Learning is Not All in Your Head.** Great Ocean Publishers, VA 1995

Jensen, Eric. **Brain Based Learning.** Turning Point, CA 1996

Kline, Peter. **The Everyday Genius.** Great Ocean Publishers, VA 1988

Oech, Roger von, Ph.D. **A Whack on the Side of the Head.** Warner Books, NY 1983

Oech, Roger von. Ph.D. **A Kick in the Seat of the Pants.** Harper & Row, NY 1986

Rose, Colin. **Accelerated Learning for the Twentieth Century.** Dell Publishing, NY 1997

Vance, Mike. **Think Out of the Box.** Career Press, NJ 1997

Venolia, Carol. **Healing Environments.** Celestial Arts, CA 1988

Williams, Linda. **Teaching for the Two-Sided Mind.** Simon and Schuster, NY 1983

Books for Trainers:

• • • • •

Accelerated Learning CourseBuilder. The Center for Accelerated Learning, WI 1999 (414-248-7070)

Bowman, Sharon. *How To Give It So They Get It.* Bowperson Publishing, NV 1998 (775-749-5247)

Bowman, Sharon. *Presenting with Pizzazz.* Bowperson Publishing, NV 1997

Charles, G. Leslie and Clarke-Epstein, Chris. *The Instant Trainer.* McGraw-Hill, NY 1998 (715-842-2467)

Floyd, Elaine. *Marketing with Newletters.* Newsletter Resources, 1997 (800-264-6305)

Foster, Elizabeth, Ed.D. *Energizers and Icebreakers.* Educational Media Corporation, MN 1989

Gesell, Izzy. *Playing Along.* Whole Person Associates, MN 1997

Miller, Mary and Vincent, Mary Jeanne. *Tips for Trainers.* Play Breaks, 1998 (650-802-8181)

Silberman, Mel. *101 Ways to Make Training Active.* Jossey-Bass/Pfeiffer, CA 1995

Silberman, Mel. *Active Training.* McMillan, NY 1990

Pike, Robert and Arch, Dave. *Dealing with Difficult Participants.* Jossey-Bass/Pfeiffer, CA

Pike, Robert. *Creative Training Techniques Handbook.* Lakewood Books, MN 1994

Slan, Joanna. *Using Stories and Humor: Grab Your Audience.* Allyn & Bacon, MA 1998 (800-356-2220)

Thiagarajan, Sivasailam. *Facilitators Tool Kit.* (812-332-1478)